LITERATURE WITH A SMALL 'L'

DEVELOPING THINKING SKILLS IN LANGUAGE TEACHING AND LEARNING

JOHN MCRAE

WAYZGOOSE PRESS

3rd edition: Wayzgoose Press, 2022.

ISBN: 978-1938757914

Edited by Dorothy Zemach

Cover design by DJ Rogers for Bookbranders

First published as *Literature with a Small 'l'* as an MEP Monograph, by Macmillan, Basingstoke, UK, in 1991.

Second edition published as *Creative Reading and Literature with a Small 'l'*, by Anvil Press, Manila, 2008.

CONTENTS

PREFACE

In future years, the absence of imaginative content in language teaching will be considered to have marked a primitive stage of the discipline: the use of purely referential materials limits the learner's imaginative involvement with the target language and leads to a one-dimensional learning achievement. Representational materials make an appeal to the learner's imagination: they can be any kind of material with imaginative or fictional content that goes beyond the purely referential, and brings imaginative interaction, reaction and response into play.

In the context of second language learning and teaching, literature has usually tended to have a capital 'L'. The principal aim of this book is to get rid of that institutionalising capital, and to show, in practical rather than theoretical terms, how literature is both necessary and useful in language teaching.

This approach sees literature in the widest possible sense of the word: representational and ideational materials of all periods, styles and forms are covered. The all-purpose term 'literature' has provoked much philosophical examination, summed up in Jean-

Paul Sartre's title, *What is Literature?* A reductive answer, for the purposes of this book, might be 'any text whose imaginative content will stimulate reaction and response in the receiver'.

Children learn to use language through invention, experimentation and stories: the language they use is very rapidly related to imaginative stimuli, whether these be in the form of games (dolls or toy soldiers who take on a fictional existence), nursery rhymes and play-songs, fairy tales and comics, TV series or computer games. The words used are made to play, to have representational meaning beyond their limited sphere of literal reference. It is this phenomenon that I have called 'wordsplay', and I see it as practically relevant in L2 learning and teaching at all levels, using as stimuli 'literature' materials of all kinds.

Basically, the thesis of this book is that language learning through the use of representational and ideational materials can and should go hand in hand with the learning of referential uses of language, and the concomitant study of grammar and the mechanisms of the target language. In using the terms 'representational' and 'ideational', I am, in fact, making free with Jakobson's six functions of language, and compressing several non-referential functions into two all-purpose adjectives. They are intended as terms that can be used in language teaching rather than identifications of specific functions of language.

This is principally to facilitate discussion. Linguistics and linguistic descriptions of texts are beyond the scope of the present book, whose concern is largely with the practice of language teaching and the use of what might very loosely be described as imaginative texts in second language learning and teaching.

Students of linguistics will find much to disagree with, and language teachers may want to go more deeply into some of the theoretical questions this book does little more than touch upon. There are several excellent books which cover the ground that this book either takes for granted or skirts round—some of these are indicated in the bibliography. Language teaching is a magpie business, and no apology is due for the appropriation of ideas from other fields, although, of course, their application will always be open to discussion.

PREAMBLE

McRae signals a new era in language teaching which will be characterized by "the fuller integration of the text into teaching, the mixing of representational with referential, the development of language awareness concurrently with knowledge about language.

Judit Zerkowitz (2006)

WHEN *LITERATURE WITH A SMALL l* WAS FIRST PUBLISHED, IN 1991, it raised a range of issues about the language/literature interface, about literature in language teaching, and about referential *versus* representational language. These reached a wide audience, and were discussed worldwide. Many of the ideas in the book were implemented at various levels, from official Ministerial programmes and curricula to individual teachers using imaginative materials in their classrooms.

Ten years after the last edition of the book became available, in autumn 2007, I was asked, with Amos Paran, to lead an online

IATEFL fielded discussion on the topic of literature in language teaching—and lo and behold, precisely the same range of questions, issues, doubts, fears, assertions and success stories emerged again.

Little has changed in the field of education, and this should neither surprise nor disappoint us. There have been a great many developments, new ideas, refinements, theories and a few new practices. But fundamentally these are all questions of enhanced awareness rather than radical shifts. The basic purpose of what we are doing remains the same, and always will: the teaching of language in the most effective and rewarding ways. For myself, that effectiveness and satisfaction derives from the development of five skills, rather than the traditional four—the skill of thinking being the added element which imaginative, representational texts can bring to the process.

Along the way there have been occasional voices raised against the use of literature in language teaching, and these viewpoints must not be ignored. They can be summarised under various headings: that literature is irrelevant to our students; that literature is difficult and unrepresentative of "normal" language use; that literature involves different skills from the language skills we should be teaching; and that literature represents some kind of post-imperial value system which would be a cultural imposition on our learners.

All of these have been addressed in published responses over the years: Amos Paran sensibly dismisses much of this kind of reasoning in his 2008 overview in the *English Language Teaching Journal*, which, with *Language and Literature*, the journal of the Poetics and Linguistics Association, gives an excellent regular (usually annual) overview of work in the field.

If I may summarise the responses rapidly, I would have to insist simply that they all share a misconception about what literature is —and they tend to start from the presupposition that we are talking about Literature (capital L) and go on from there. Literature is indeed a vital specialist subject (see Chapter 11 of this book), but we are talking more significantly about *representational texts and materials*, which I argue are literature with a small l, a long way from the field of Literature, which such critics perceive as specialist, and indeed elitist.

The upshot is that readers of such negative articles often take fright and flee from the whole subject area because they do not consider themselves Literature specialists, perhaps because they were taught Literature so badly themselves or because they never enjoyed it as a subject. Thus the negative stance becomes a self-fulfilling prophesy.

By way of contrast with this, in seminars and workshops in many countries time and again I have seen the scales fall from participants' eyes as they realise how wide a range of imaginative materials literature with a small l can offer. T.S. Eliot, no less, famously said, "immature poets imitate, mature poets steal". In the same way, the mature teacher is a magpie, and steals shame-lessly any materials that might prove useful in any particular class in any particular context.

And that material can range, notoriously but excitingly, from bus tickets, to soft drinks cans, to advertisements, to popular songs, newspaper articles, cartoons—and on to the more tradition-ally literary forms that might include extended prose, poems, plays, from any period or any context. Anything that can be read can be grist to the mill. The songs mentioned in the first edition still work—and of course there have been thousands more since then.

That is the range. Any kind of imaginative material that a reader can process is grist to the mill. Problems teachers might have are more likely to be problems of their own resistance rather than problems of accessibility or of student resistance.

A good teacher will choose material that is suitable for his or her students—"difficulty" is often only in the teacher's own mind, and is part of the resistance. As soon as that resistance is broken down, the new convert frequently becomes the most enthusiastic proponent of work at the lang/lit interface. This can happen at the institutional level just as much as it can at the individual level: governments and ministries of education which have proved resistant over the years are now seeing more and more the visible, verifiable benefit of working systematically with imaginative materials in the language classroom, for all subject areas where English is required. This is not luxury teaching: its way of working is fundamentally in tune with how the human brain works. Recent developments in cognitive science have backed up what previously was imagined, to paraphrase William Blake.

Because it is *not* a specialist historical or critical study, the use of representational literature materials in language teaching needs no literary background, no specialist knowledge. Any teacher who is methodologically aware and can teach language communicatively can teach Five Skills English. It is simply a question of going beyond the limitations of referential materials and traditional language teaching texts.

Comprehension is a starting-point here, rather than a point of arrival. Intelligent content and relevant input are stimuli to thinking, and this leads on to spoken and written output. That this does produce more able readers and better users of the target language has now been the subject of a considerable body of academic study: Masters dissertations and doctoral theses in several countries over two decades. Both statistical and empirical results are overwhelmingly positive, and have given Ministries the confidence to implement representational or langlit programmes in many contexts. The critical mass is accumulating.

An unexpected kind of resistance, but on a pretty small scale, has come from Literature teachers themselves, who might at first not appreciate how a linguistic approach to literary texts enhances and enriches the teaching/learning experience. In a world where web access means teachers are no longer the only source of informational input about authors and periods, the teacher has more space to work directly with the text and encourage students to work autonomously on researching aspects which previously might have had to be given as input. Language awareness, text awareness and cultural awareness are now in the literature teacher's standard armoury, just as literature is now becoming a more and more recognised part of the language teacher's bank of resources.

There is a process of democratization at work here—literature of all kinds is becoming more and more accessible to a wider range of readers.

Literature with a Small 'l' then and now

A long time has passed since the ideas expressed in this book were first formulated. Since then, as we have said, the ideas have been put into practice in a wide range of contexts all over the world. They have grown, developed, matured, been adapted and been applied with gratifying results. Above all, they have been proved to work, and that is why it is time to look at them again, critically and constructively, to see where things stand now and where they seem to be heading in the field of representational and referential materials, literature with a small l, and what has come to be known more and more as Five Skills English.

The ability to think critically about language and text has come to be recognised as an integral part of language education. *Critical thinking* and its terminology are now applied in many areas—asking the right questions, evaluating issues and formulating responses are part of a great many intellectual and educational disciplines. The use of representational materials in language teaching is, I would suggest, a practical application of critical thinking methods.

Advocates of critical thinking strongly believe that there is an intimate relationship between language, identity, power and intercultural relations. The belief is that language and reality construct each other, that language creates ideas and values and it changes dynamically according to different contexts. Therefore, the analysis of the language of the text and of how meaning is created by words is fundamental to the making of meaning of the text; and similarly vital is the analysis of how texts are read by individuals and groups in their contexts.

A lot of recent research, culminating in two major books by Ronald Carter and Rob Pope, has emphasized how *creativity* has come to be seen as a natural part of language use. This is something that seems to be an inbuilt human capacity, and ties in with the work of popular academics like Steven Pinker. We will look more deeply into this in the next section.

However, in many ways language teaching has been conditioned by how language learning is tested. In the first edition of *Literature with a Small 'l'*, I outlined very sketchily in Chapter 10 some basic notions on testing and evaluation. Sadly these have often been taken as some kind of prescriptive gospel, whereas they were and remain only tentative points for discussion, starting-points for experiment.

Some very good work has been carried out in the field, but the area of literary "competence" remains one that needs to be researched more deeply and scientifically. There always remain the twin dangers of "competitive sensitivity" (i.e., "I am more sensitive than you; therefore I appreciate literature better than you do") and the quantitative scientific analysis of elements of a text, usually specific linguistic items, which can lead to conclusions about the text itself but give no indication of the reader's ways of reading or understanding the text on a wider scale. A balance between subjectivity and objectivity has to be the aim.

In several contexts where an integrated language and literature approach has been implemented at Ministerial level, good research has been undertaken into such questions as band descriptors, how to evaluate the language used in relation to the content of the response, and the whole question of the balance between subjectivity and objectivity in literature evaluation. However, a great deal remains to be done, and we await some major contributions to scientific research in the field.

One of the most significant advances in the study of language and language-learning has been work on descriptive grammars of the language as it is spoken, of language use as documented in computer corpora.

This has given us new insights into the old questions of use and usage, and reinforced the necessity for educators and learners to be aware not only of *prescriptive* grammar with its rules and ways of working, but of the *descriptive* grammar which documents and illustrates the language as a living, constantly-changing resource, working within rules, with rules and beyond rules. Recent innovative grammar teaching books have shown that creativity can sit very successfully with what used to be considered the chore of grammar learning and teaching.

The cliché that "rules are made to be broken" has been amply confirmed by this kind of work, and therefore makes it all the more important that teachers and learners have an adequate set of guidelines to work with when they are examining how a text means. The headings in the checklist (see page 00) of *register*, *period*, and *function* become all the more clearly significant in the context of whatever kind of English is being read. These take us well beyond the vocabulary and grammar under the headings of *lexis* and *syntax*: these are only the tip of the iceberg. And it has to be stressed this can be an older form of English (*period*) just as much as a newer English from a range of different geographical areas.

Under the heading of *dialect* in the checklist I intended to accommodate questions of standard and non-standard English, which in the early 90s were still the subject of discussion under such headings as "deviation" in some quarters.

The map of World Englishes has changed considerably in the meantime, and the ever-widening range of Englishes available to us has now come to be seen as a resource, rather than a problem. "Rotten English", as Ken Saro-Wiwa called it in the subtitle of his great novel *Sozaboy*, is now almost as much a part of literature in English as standard English used to be. Incidentally, some political correctness objections have been raised to a quotation in Chapter 7 under the sub-heading of "culture and shock" where the word "nigger" is used in a quotation from 1924; it is followed by a much more recent quotation about gay-bashing, which has not provoked any outrage whatsoever! Both make something clear about point of view, and both make a point about prejudice in its manifold forms. The reaction and response are up to the reader, as ever.

One major difference nowadays in the materials that would be used in the teaching of literature with a small l is a considerably enhanced range of texts from "new" Englishes from all over the world, and this is greatly to be welcomed. Writing in English is no longer the property even of native-English speaking writers: as David Graddol has shown us in his research for the British Council, there are more non-native users of English than native-speakers worldwide, and the implications for old-fashioned concepts of linguistic imperialism and so on are enormous. English is a world language because it is used worldwide by an increasing number of speakers and writers; as a global language of communication its status has changed. This is what has now come to be called English as a lingua franca.

Going beyond: from stylistics to cognitive poetics, text world theory, and onwards

Many steps forward have been taken in the past twenty years in the academic field of textual study through linguistic practices—the study of corpora, text world theory, cognitive poetics, critical discourse analysis, conceptual blending, and others have added immensely to our awareness of how cognitive processes work. Language Awareness has become almost a discipline in itself, with a journal of that very title. Many of the most useful works in several of these areas are listed in the bibliography, (which is intended to be selective rather than exhaustive), with a view to indicating titles which readers of the present volume are more likely to find instructive.

In some cases, textual analysis has become something of an end in itself. But one of the leading figures in the field, and one if its most consistent practitioners, Mick Short, put his finger on the main focus of what we are doing when he said, introducing a stylistic approach to reading a text (1995: 53):

> Stylistic analysis, unlike more traditional forms of practical criticism, is not interested primarily in coming up with new and startling interpretations of the texts it examines. Rather, its main aim is to explicate how our understanding of a text is achieved, by examining in detail the linguistic organization of the texts and how a reader needs to interact with the linguistic organization to make sense of it.

This emphasis on language and how it works ties in precisely and fully with what we are doing with representational materials in a language teaching and learning context. Short goes on to add that "often, such a detailed examination of a text does reveal new aspects of interpretation or help us to see more clearly how a text achieves what it does. But the main purpose of stylistics is to show how interpretation is achieved, and hence provide support for a particular view of the work under discussion."

This seems to me to open the way to any critical or historical approach to any text, literary or not, canonical or not. "How interpretation is achieved" is the point of critical reading and thinking about texts, whether we call it stylistics, old-fashioned practical criticism, creative reading, appreciation, or whatever.

The "particular view" of any text under discussion can be a simple as an initial subjective response to reading an imaginative text in the target language (or indeed in one's own language). The toolbox that our checklist provides can be applied at any level of language or literary or cultural study, with any degree of sophistication from almost uninitiated to expert.

It is in this context that we have to remind ourselves that for our present purposes the focus is pedagogic. We are teaching language and teaching reading. Often the context is second or foreign language learning (but by no means exclusively—the principles apply to all reading in all language learning contexts). We are also sometimes teaching literature, with both a small and a capital L, and it is a basic premise of this book that these two "sides" of literature study are interdependent, inseparable, and united at every point by the language of the text. Literature study without language awareness is now widely seen as inappropriate, if not anathema.

Of course there remain divisions within English Departments between the "language" side of things and the "literature" side. These will gradually evaporate, and silly questions like "Are you more of a literature person or more of a language person?", with their hint of implied snobbery, will become even more meaningless than they are now.

Fundamentally text is text, and the first thing we have to do is read the text. What we do with it thereafter and where we take the level of study—critical, theoretical, linguistic, cultural, historical, contextual, socio-political—will in each case involve specialist skills and approaches. But this move towards specialisation cannot and must not diminish the enormous contribution of those educators who handle the basic first principles of the approach. That contribution has often been undervalued, but it is where the most basically important steps have to be taken, and is in some senses where educators have the greatest responsibility.

Where a couple of decades ago we had a range of philosophical and linguistic theories at our disposal (structuralism, deconstruction, Marxism, new historicism, feminism and post-feminism, etc.), and learned to become highly eclectic in our appropriation of useful lessons from them, we today have a not dissimilar range of approaches, philosophies and textual strategies which frequently have a more linguistic basis. These can be of immense benefit to the highly selective teacher who is keen to explore new ways of reading, processing and thinking about texts in order then to transfer this knowledge to the teaching context. *Pedagogical stylistics* is one label that has attached itself to his general area, but it covers a wide range of disciplines, and every teacher will make an individual decision about the usefulness of any one approach.

We cannot do it all, and should not try to. Teachers are busy people, but we have an endless curiosity about what might help us to do our job better. We have to follow our curiosity and our instincts, and not be seduced by what is momentarily fashionable. Above all, what helps us teach better, and what helps our students learn better, must be our watchwords.

Creativity and language learning

One of the many developments in the scientific study of language over the at two decades has been a growing emphasis on human creativity in language, with a focus on our capacity to use languages, to think beyond limited ranges, to exploit the vast range of human words to make an infinite number of sentences and discourses.

For the general reader the work of Jean Aitchison and Steven Pinker has expanded on the seminal work by Lakoff and Johnson,

Metaphors We Live By, which opened up the ground between representational and referential language decisively in 1980.

Creativity has become a buzzword in language studies, and is slowly being assimilated into language teaching and learning contexts through such excellent books as those already mentioned by Ronald Carter and Rob Pope (see the bibliography).

These two writers, who happen to be both innovative and accomplished scholars as well as excellent practising teachers, have documented how human beings use their natural capacity to express themselves, in everyday language use, well beyond the restrictions of mere transactional, referential communication. We have what Pinker and others would argue is an inborn capacity, often expressed through metaphor and other analogies, which enables us to grasp and manage very complex concepts and abstractions, and relate them to our everyday human experience.

This is a question of being able to *conceptualise*, and it is this capacity which enables us to handle problematic issues of time and space, of the finite and the infinite, of cause and effect, of causation and agency, of abstract concepts such as beauty and terror.

We have words that can encompass every kind of reality, and a great many fictional realities as well. English has more vocabulary items available to its users than most other languages—but the language stock, our word hoard, although ever-expanding, is finite. However, as we suggested above, the possible combinations we can make when we put words together are almost infinite.

Yet, of course, they are bounded by rules—not simply grammatical rules, but collocations, usages, ways of handling language which are recognisable as acceptable, or which can be exploited for their surprise value, their breaking with standard practice. Pinker's famous example which contrasts "fill a glass with water" and (not possible) "pour a glass with water" is a fine case in point here—and we could go on forever with such examples.

Is there a "rule" which governs why we cannot say "fill water into a glass" but we can use "pour water into a glass"? I would suggest there is something logical here—to "fill" is an action which when completed means the glass is full; pour suggests merely the action without going as far as the consequence, and without going into the equally thorny question of whether the glass is half full or half empty when the action is completed.

In my experience, all languages are representational, creative, and expanding. Naturally some are more so than others, and some cultures simply do not connect with the English propensity for puns and wordplay. Wittgenstein's famous assertion "it is only in a language that I can mean something by something" has to be mentioned here. Because, in using words themselves, we have chosen a means of meaning something *by* the use of words; we can mean something by a gesture, an expression or a look, a sigh, an action—this is where drama begins. But mostly we use language together with these more physical ways of expressing ourselves. We can mean by silence too—a taxonomy of types of silence would be immense too, as every silence in every context might mean something different.

When *Literature with a Small l* was first published, many of these discussions and debates were at an early stage. I make no claims to prescience, but it does seem that the necessity to bring representational language into language teaching is all the more evident today than it was in 1991, partly because of the impact of so much recent research and scientific argument.

And recent work on the grammar of English has confirmed all these arguments, and in doing so, caused further debate. As we have seen, it is a vitally important step forward that we are now consulting *descriptive* grammars, which document examples of the language in use, rather than only using the prescriptive kind of grammar book which set down the rules. Language teaching has to work between the two. Language teaching always has to allow for variables.

Clearly there are grammatical ways of working which are more acceptably widespread than others. Normally in English the verb follows the subject—but not always. Normally in English the third person singular of a verb has a final -s—but not always. And so on.

Many teachers remain trapped in an old-fashioned belief that "grammar" is the bottom line, the ultimate safety net which might also be a security blanket. I have often been asked, for example, "Can I use literature to teach grammar?" or "What is the place of grammar in literature teaching?" And I find it difficult to answer such questions, because behind them is a kind of hopeful (possibly desperate) assumption that grammar can provide all the answers. It cannot, nor should it.

It was in order to get out of the grammar trap that my original check-list of language features which teachers can use in the teaching of representational materials was first put together. And that was done with considerable help from applied linguists, grammarians and teachers. Perhaps surprisingly to some, the checklist works. Its intention is very clearly not to be exhaustive in its listing of features such as morphology (between lexis and syntax, if you like) pragmatics (under register, I would suggest) and other familiar linguistic features beloved of teachers of a certain kind everywhere.

The checklist is intended to focus attention of the features of the language which can help readers, students, learners to negotiate with texts, to evaluate *how* texts mean rather than merely what they mean—to enable them to become better, more aware, more competent readers of imaginative materials, and, as has been proved in a considerable number of research projects in many countries and contexts, better and more aware users of the language.

Five Skills English – the heart of the matter

This section encapsulates many of the arguments which are more widely discussed in the original *Literature with a Small 'l'*. They are summarised here, at the risk of repeating things and of restating the obvious, in order to set out the ground, anticipating some of the discussions in the main body of the book, and to relate the current situation in English language teaching to the basics of the representational, five skills approach. In order to illustrate the theory in practical terms, we will look at some texts, both "literary" and not, in order to see how reading awareness can be developed and something of Culler's posited "progress as readers of literature" quoted below, can be achieved.

The four skills approach to communicative language teaching has been with us for a long time. It is not perfect, but in many ways it is seen as the best and most effective way of teaching English as a Second or Foreign Language.

Listening, speaking, reading and writing are taught as separate or integrated skills, and are tested in ways which allow for right and wrong answers, and grades which confirm a target level of achievement reached. It is usually possible to get 100% correct answers in most language tests.

This indicates that the testing system is predominantly closed, rather than open in its choices and variables. Progress in language learning is seen as measurable, quantifiable, in terms of language items, lexical items, structures etc. acquired, produced, recognised and manipulated.

As long ago as 1977 Jonathan Culler wrote (quoted also in Chapter 6):

> Our examinations are not designed merely to check whether (a student) has read and remembered certain books but to test his or her progress as a reader of literature.

This statement was made in the context of the teaching of literature with a small "l", and uses highly debatable terminology with regard to the subject of testing and evaluation. However, its basic thrust is very significant and merits reflection on the question of progress as a learner of language, and the abilities and skills that are required of language learners after the so-called communicative language teaching "revolution."

There is a distinction to be drawn here between *testing* and *evaluation* of learners' progress. *Testing* suggests a closed system of right/wrong, stating with a concept of all correct answers and taking marks off, *evaluation* a more open system, perhaps starting from zero and rewarding the candidate.

In large part, the language system that is taught in the four skills approach focuses on *referential* language. This is language which means exactly what it says, where one word has one meaning, and where grammar and syntax follow the accepted rules. It is a rule-based approach, and usefully gives a basis for language use, a linguistic skeleton which learners can move on to fleshing out.

However, the four skills approach frequently ignores *representational* language. That is language which is open to interpretation, contains plurality of meaning potential rather than one single denotational meaning, and requires negotiation and judgment by its receiver in order to be fully understood.

No living language in the world can remain only at the referential level for very long. Every language in use is hugely representational, and perhaps no language more so than English.

Most communicative language teaching is based on an assumed idealised communicative situation where interlocutors say what they mean and mean what they say, and are received and understood as such. This is fine for communicative practice simulation. But, as the work of Deborah Tannen and others has shown, this assumption is patently false in the world outside the classroom.

Recent work on corpora of spoken English goes a long way to

confirming that language in use is rarely as prescriptive and definitive as the kind of language learned in a communicative methodology. English in use is hedged about with modality, with vague language, with hesitations and lack of commitment, whereas learners of English are usually encouraged to use definite verbs, assertion, affirmation. The use of "may" or "might" is simply not sufficiently widespread in current language teaching: it is the first major step towards a mastery of the enabling language required for discussion, the statement of views, opinions etc.

It is this that leads to the necessity for a fifth skill to be incorporated into the currently widespread four skills communicative approach to language teaching and learning.

The fifth skill is the skill of *processing* and *thinking*. Any text spoken, written, or heard has to be processed and thought about in order that its implications be decoded, its frame of reference understood, its context and connotations assimilated, its ideological standpoints assessed, where it is coming from and who it is directed at, all being incorporated into the overall understanding.

Comprehension is widely perceived, especially by learners, as the ultimate aim, the point of arrival, the main target of learning achievement. This is a misapprehension both of how language works and of what language acquisition and proficiency are all about.

Where the four skills approach has tended to focus on *comprehension* as a testable aim, the five skills approach sees comprehension as a starting-point, point zero in the processing of the text, whether it be spoken or written.

Five skills offers a *process-based* rather than a *product-based* approach. Experience of the language and how it works is frequently seen as more significant than information. Of course, information transfer on a purely referential level is vitally important in many fields of communication and language use. But it is limited in its applications to specialised areas of, particularly, professional language use.

Referential texts and representationality – texts with attitude

Even a text which purports to be referential, such as a dictionary entry, lends itself to fruitful processing. The following text is, as the graphology shows, a dictionary entry:

> **Beans on toast**
>
> is a popular snack, eaten at any time of the day. Heinz, the most popular brand of baked beans, originally canned beans in tomato sauce in 1895, and when they were imported into Britain a few years later they were sold as an expensive luxury. Everyone can afford their beans now and many companies sell them. Heinz alone sells approximately 2,500,000 cans every day.
>
> See *Snack*.

What students can be invited to see in this text is some sort of ideological construct: *who* is writing and *to whom* becomes a highly useful question. The apparatus would concentrate on *where* the text's frame of reference covers (it is wholly British-centred), *how much* information is given for anyone who knows nothing about the subject (colour, size and type of beans are not mentioned, toast is never mentioned). Frequently students read this as a veiled advertisement for Heinz, as it seems to stress the brand name more than might seem necessary. Questions such as "Who is 'everyone'?" also reveal something about the assumptions the text (and possibly its producer) make. The fact that at current supermarket prices in the UK Heinz beans cost three times the price of a supermarket's own economy brand might give another insight to the question.

Contrasting that text with a genuine advertising slogan for the same company and product illuminates useful differences in graphology, syntax, semantics and function:

BEANZ MEANZ HEINZ

Students need encouragement to "see through language" in this way, but as soon as they realise that it is fruitful and indeed fun, they take to it rapidly and can be encouraged to read any text, from newspapers to text-books, from the non-literary text through any kind of literature (with a small 'l' or a large 'L') with a healthy questioning attitude. With well-written texts this will of course lead to a greater appreciation of the text's qualities and the effects it achieves.

This works with *any* kind of text and discourse: advertising is widely used in language teaching; newspapers which present widely different perspectives on the same story, political discourse, agony aunts—any text that might represent a point of view, or have an agenda, or want to influence the reader in some way. Any and all of these and many more are grist to the mill, because they represent the reader with a challenge, with something to find out —these are all *texts with attitude*.

The development of the fifth skill, and the acquisition of processing skills, involves a refining of three levels of awareness in cognitive terms:

language awareness
text awareness
cultural awareness

The fifth skill is in itself nothing new: it effectively embodies the three ways of learning language originally outlined by Halliday when he suggested that a three-part structure is needed for discussions of language learning:

learning language
learning through language
learning about language

The most innovative recent textbooks and the best practice over recent years have implicitly been incorporating materials which require interpretation skills. and which expand cultural awareness as well as developing the basic language skills.

What is to be learned is twofold: the mechanisms of the syntax of the target language are a more or less *closed* system, with not too many variables, a system of syntax which has more or less clear rules of use and usage. Then there is the much more open system of lexis and register, which necessarily involves *choice* on the part of the producer of the language and *a capacity to evaluate and respond* to that series of choices on the part of the receiver.

The factors which condition such choices are of course manifold: they are social, cultural, linguistic, ideological, historical, local, personal, affective, and can indeed be as idiosyncratic as the individual speaker. Communicative language teaching and learning have, almost by necessity, avoided too much consideration of these factors, in a justifiable attempt to streamline the learning to what is quantifiable, and can be standardised.

At various times there have been debates on linguistic competence, fluency *versus* accuracy, the differences between written and spoken English. and the vexed question of standard and non-standard English. These will no doubt continue. Their relevance to the present discussion is considerable.

The new element which Five Skills English brings to bear on these debates is the concentration on how the language works rather than what it says: on *how* it means rather than simply on *what* it means.

Binaries are often the best simple lead-in to the dynamic of how a text means—binaries between, for example, "I" and "you", before and after, life and death, good and bad, male and female, night and day, past and present, present and future, often very simply give the reader something to latch on to, give the student something to talk about immediately. Here is an example from a poem which can be read as canonical, or simply as an attractive, approachable text

> *Little Fly,*
> *Thy summer's play*
> *My thoughtless hand*
> *Has brush'd away.*
>
> *Am not I*
> *A fly like thee?*
> *Or art not thou*
> *A man like me?*
>
> *For I dance,*
> *And drink, & sing,*
> *Till some blind hand*
> *Shall brush my wing.*
>
> *If thought is life*
> *And strength & breath,*
> *And the want*
> *Of thought is death;*
>
> *Then am I*
> *A happy fly.*
> *If I live*
> *Or if I die.*

This text, in deceptively simple language, offers a wonderful series of binaries: I/thee, man/fly, life/death, and later, thought/want of thought—to name but the most obvious ones. It also offers stanza by stanza a movement from present perfect, through present, to future and on to the final two stanzas which are conditioned by the repeated word "If". Textual intervention means we could take away the final two stanzas to see what happens—it clearly becomes a very different text.

It also moves from narration of a past event in the first stanza, to questioning, and on to reasoning and then the conditional clauses—all this movement allows for the more "literary" themes to emerge if the class wants to go there. And historically William Blake's classic binary of innocent/experience can come into play as well, moving the text on into its historical context in the socio-political sphere of the time of its writing and indeed its place in the history of English literature. But for a basic reading of the text there is no need to go this far. The text can be a simple reading experience, albeit with quite complex ideas, it can be an introduction to some of the complexities of what is known as the Romantic period, or of the aftermath of the French revolution in England, it can represent something of man/nature as a binary of identification and sympathy—the range of interpretative possibilities is well-nigh endless.

This is to illustrate that a single text can be taken anywhere, according to the needs, wants and abilities of the readers in the teaching situation. It can be a text to be read, enjoyed, thought about and discussed in class—or it can be an approach to the specialised subject of the history of literature: these are ends of the same spectrum, and only as distant from each other as the teacher wants to make them.

Against reading comprehension

I once had a class tackle a First Certificate in English (FCE) Reading Comprehension, but made the mistake of omitting to give them the passage to read: they only had the questions.

They all passed.

Replicating this accidental but revealing mistake deliberately for research purposes in several teaching contexts, I found that the results more or less replicated themselves: no-one got 100% correct answers. But with the application of a little intelligence, a process of elimination and some guess-work it was easy for a pass level to be achieved. This suggested to me that Reading Comprehension in that particular form was effectively testing *neither* reading *nor* comprehension. What students had learned to do was apply some mechanical techniques to a testing situation in order to get a satisfactory result.

Of course. this is anecdotal rather than scientific evidence and I use it only to describe a seminal classroom experience. But is often from our mistakes and failures that we gain our most useful insights.

The question that arises is, simply, how valuable is comprehension in and of itself? How much is reading comprehension applicable to a text such as this one, a text which has been widely used in representational language teaching textbooks:

40 – LOVE

40 –	love
middle	aged
couple	playing
ten	nis
when	the
game	ends
and	they
go	home
the	net
will	still
be	be
tween	them

It is almost impossible to consider this text in the usual class-room context of comprehension. Rather, it requires *processing*. The "traditional" question "What is it about?" might not be as fatuous as it may seem. Answers could cover a range of ideas, from tennis to relationships, from marriage to graphology.

The point would emerge, however, that the text is not only about one thing: it is as much about the themes that might arise from discussion as it is about the text itself, its layout and its form reflecting the nature of the subject-matter and content. It will be about different things for different people. A fifteen-year-old will react differently from a forty-year-old. As with most representa-tional texts, it is difficult to be prescriptive about there being one correct answer. To quote George Eliot, "all meaning lies in the key of interpretation."

The kind of apparatus used in working with a text like *40 — Love* could involve questions as above, and such textual interven-tion strategies as rewriting: if the text is rewritten in sentence form it loses much of its impact, and indeed its meaning.

This is yet again a useful confirmation of one of the main points

I feel needs to be reiterated: the importance of *how* a text means, going beyond *what* it means.

Similarly the effect or *function* of the texts can be explored by inviting students to discuss appropriate adjectives to describe the text and it impact—the following might be suggested "sad, witty, clever, amusing, disconcerting," or, "not really poetry." Of course readers may opt for others, for more than one of these, and may even dislike and react against the text.

Another aspect of the text which might attract learner interest is the etymology of the word "love" meaning zero in a tennis score: it comes from the French *l'oeuf* since it would appear that tennis was originally scored with a kind of abacus with egg-shaped balls, one of which represented the score of zero. (Of course, the reason might simply be that one of the balls was egg-shaped!)

It is also worth asking students what lines appeal to them most: "be be" is often chosen, partly because of the surprise dividing of the word "between"; "ten nis" is often chosen because of a similar verbal/visual effect.

In terms of grammar, the text moves the tenses of the verb from present continuous, through present (representing the future) to future. It is a recurring feature of representational texts that the tenses of the verbs show some dynamic of movement, often involving past, present and future.

The virtue of a text like this in the communicative language teaching context lies precisely in its openness, in the text's demand on its readers that it be processed on its own merits, with the reader bringing to the text shared knowledge, familiarity/unfamiliarity with culture, context, and subject-matter, language awareness, text awareness and cultural awareness. How the reader reacts depends on individual response rather than on the precise correctness of an expected answer.

Even the word "love" is called into question, which is useful if the learner knows only one meaning of the word. The source of the

meaning of "zero" as illustrated above might also be part of the
learning aims of work with this text. Learning *about* language thus
becomes part and parcel of learning the language itself. This particular poem is of course the kind of text which most easily exempli-
fies the teachability of representational texts, which is perhaps why
it is so widely used in representational textbooks.

But many students would find themselves in difficulty if asked
to respond to such a text, because they have not been trained to
produce such openness of response, and lack the confidence to
respond .

However, *any text* requires processing in not dissimilar ways.
Most texts do not have one single meaning: they require some
kind of processing, whether they be information or opinion,
prescriptive or descriptive, fiction or fact, newspaper or recipe
book. And learners have to be enabled to develop response strategies to the ever-expanding range of open texts the modern world
presents them with: from advertisements to political speeches,
from newspaper articles to song lyrics, from tourist brochures to
comics, the representationality of the language used demands a
capacity for processing, evaluating and responding to that
language.

As suggested earlier, the *enabling language* which students
require in order to be able to discuss the processing they carry out
with texts is the language of modality, of "might" and "may", of
opinion and possibility, rather than certainty and right/wrong
answers.

Of course it can be unsettling for learners to be deprived of the
security blanket of there being a right or a wrong answer—but
moving beyond that restricted referential level is a vital step
forward in progress as a language learner. The analogy is of a driver
learning to drive and never moving out of first gear.

Until recently the jump from referential language learning to an
awareness of representationality in the language teaching context

has been left to a late stage in the proceedings, if it has been faced at all.

Teachers have to begin the awareness raising process as early as possible in the language learning career of the student: left too late, bridging that gap becomes progressively more difficult. If representational materials are introduced *from the very earliest stages* of language learning, the learner's imagination is called into play, there is an awareness that judgment and response are part of language development, and a confidence is built that the learner *does* have something worth saying, something to bring to the text, some personal contribution to offer, rather than simply being at the mercy of the materials and the teaching of an unknown subject.

Around the world now, in the context of language-teaching textbook research and writing, several areas have already emerged where process-based representational methodology can be applied. These applications and points to consider include the following:

- Materials selection: where texts come from, when they were written;
- Are they examples of current English? Spoken or written, or a mix of registers?
- Are they British, American or another local English?
- Techniques of reading such as the finding of binaries and opposites, and following through of verb tenses to find the movement of the text, individual cohesive features which create phoric flow, etc.
- If translation is used. how does the text translate into the learner's own current language, or back from that language into current English? Contrastive language awareness of how *both* languages work is fundamental to process-based methodology.
- Continuous variation of question-types is necessary: from lower-order to higher-order questions, and with as

much variation in question-types as possible, according
to the requirements of the individual text;

- Formulation of questions for open response rather than
pre-determined correct answers;
- Perceptions of interpretation, ideology, and "spin"
contained within the text;
- Implicatures and cultural assumptions;
- Evaluation of lexical choice, rather than an emphasis on
vocabulary acquisition—consideration of how frequently
usable a new lexical item might be, for example.
- Learner awareness of teaching/learning outcomes
perception of the text-book as a starting-point rather
than an end-point;
- The importance of graphology, layout and visual stimuli
as part of the process of meaning creation and response;
- The question of thoroughness versus flexibility,
standardisation versus individuality;
- The evaluation of appropriateness of response: best
answers rather than single possible right answer;
- The contextualisation of closed and open choices.

Clearly all these areas merit considerable reflection and
research, and there will be many more which will emerge as work
on Five Skills methodology expands. All four currently recognised
skills will require separate work on process-based approaches, and
a priority will be the testing and evaluation system and the need to
overcome and go beyond its rather inflexible approach to correctness of response—there is, as we have seen, in the discussion of
representational texts hardly ever one correct answer.

Robert Louis Stevenson expressed the whole problematic in
glowing late-Victorian terms—but what he was saying is as true
today. Now we have the ways and means to do it for ourselves:

Conclusion.—We may now briefly enumerate the elements of style. We have, peculiar to the prose writer, the task of keeping his phrases large, rhythmical, and pleasing to the ear, without ever allowing them to fall into the strictly metrical: peculiar to the versifier, the task of combining and contrasting his double, treble, and quadruple pattern, feet and groups, logic and metre— harmonious in diversity: common to both, the task of artfully combining the prime elements of language into phrases that shall be musical in the mouth; the task of weaving their argument into a texture of committed phrases and of rounded periods—but this particularly binding in the case of prose: and, again common to both, the task of choosing apt, explicit, and communicative words. We begin to see now what an intricate affair is any perfect passage; how many faculties, whether of taste or pure reason, must be held upon the stretch to make it; and why, when it is made, it should afford us so complete a pleasure. From the arrangement of according letters, which is altogether arabesque and sensual, up to the architecture of the elegant and pregnant sentence, which is a vigorous act of the pure intellect, there is scarce a faculty in man but has been exercised. We need not wonder, then, if perfect sentences are rare, and perfect pages rarer.

I will end by quoting Clifford Geertz: "Believing with Max Weber, that man is an animal suspended in webs of significance he himself has spun, I take culture to be those webs, and the analysis of it to be, therefore, not an experimental science in search of law but an interpretative one in search of meaning."

Language and its meaning potential: that is what *Literature with a Small 'l'* was about—and what it is still about.

Now read on…

1 REPRESENTATIONAL AND REFERENTIAL

THERE IS A WIDE GAP BETWEEN THEORY AND PRACTICE in many aspects of language teaching, as is shown by frequent changes of fashion or emphasis, often led by successful textbooks. To this extent, the market is product-led. It is time this changed.

We live and work in an environment where communication has become an over-used catchword. In the era of mass communication, the age when there is a world language and that language is English, techniques of language teaching have tended to concentrate on *how* to communicate rather than on *what* to communicate *about*. Some element of communicative ability is inbuilt in humanity, and the desire or necessity to learn English reflects a wish to reach some level of communicative competence in the target language. Yet one of the most constant complaints of language learners and teachers is the lack of successful communication, often at the most basic level.

I do not wish to suggest that in advocating the use of imaginative materials in language teaching I have found the panacea that will immediately make every L2 learner fluent. Rather, I want to examine why the use of such materials is necessary, and how they should be used in the everyday context of the 'chalk-face'.

We live in a world where almost anything can be taken as a *sign*, with consequent *meanings*, which can be closed (i.e. limited or defined) or open, and which lead to inevitably wide-ranging *interpretations*. All of these areas have been the subject of exhaustive study, and the jargon consequent upon this exegesis has baffled more than a few otherwise willing readers and students.

'Text', an originally simple word, has taken on a multitude of meanings. I want to look at its usefulness in the area of second language study. I am therefore more concerned with language learning than with some closely related fields, which are, however, highly relevant to what I will say; second language acquisition, stylistics, pragmatics, applied linguistics, text linguistics and critical practices are just a few of these.

My basic question is: What is a text and what is its importance in language teaching? Dictionary definitions of 'text' take us only so far:

- the actual words of a book, poem, etc.;
- the original words of an author;
- the exact original words of any of the various forms in which a book, article, etc. exists;
- any written material.

The stress is on words, on written material. But, in the language-teaching context, illustrations, sounds, songs, advertisements, puzzles and games have all become part of a teacher's resource material. The difference between a simple stimulus to language learning and a text can be minimal: anything from a road sign to an example of modern architecture communicates a message without words. To that extent, it can be a text. The receiver of the message reacts and responds to the sign/text/meaning/ statement, in terms which can range from the purely practical (not turning left at a road sign, for example) to the aesthetic (describing a piece of modern architecture as 'a carbuncle'). 'Signs,' George Eliot wrote in Chapter 3 of *Middlemarch*, 'are small memorable things, but interpretations are illimitable.'

A text can furnish a stimulus to language learning without engaging the learner's imaginative faculties. Serious journalism, for example, presents facts and opinions as objectively as possible, without a great deal of imaginative involvement. A train ticket is just as much a text as a restaurant menu—information is conveyed in a recognisable and particular form. A painting by Monet can be read as a text, despite the dictionaries' insistence that a text contains words. A video or film, a novel or play, a poem or a love-letter—all can be read as texts.

In a language-teaching context, almost anything can be grist to the teaching/learning mill. Some texts will inevitably stimulate more language production than others, some will give information, some will give more imaginative stimuli.

This leads me to examine the difference between *referential* texts and *representational* texts, and the place of imaginative stimuli to learning. The words 'referential' and 'representational' will become key-words to the whole discussion, so it will be worth taking time out immediately to attempt to define them. As will be clear to anyone who has a familiarity with the basis of Roman Jakobson's work (1960), I am taking Jakobson's functions of language as a starting-point. (See Lodge (ed.) (1988:32-57) for the most easily available version of this paper.)

Jakobson it was who defined 'the constitutive factors in any speech event, in any act of verbal communication', as follows:

CONTEXT
ADDRESSER MESSAGE ADDRESSEE

CONTACT
CODE

These factors determine the different functions of language which Jakobson schematised as:

- Expressive
- Phatic
- Conative
- Metalingual
- Referential
- Poetic

Without wishing to go into each of these headings, or others (macro- or metafunctions, interpersonal functions, etc.) which have been derived from Jakobson's work, I want simply to make a distinction between the *referential* function, with its emphasis on description and deixis, and what I have called *representational* language.

By representational language, I mean language which, in order that its meaning potential be decoded by a receiver, engages the imagination of that receiver. There is, therefore, in representational language, something of the conative function (appealing to or influencing the addressees) and perhaps more of the metalingual and poetic functions, as Jakobson described them.

In very reductive terms, referential language is language which communicates on only one level, usually in terms of information being sought or given, or of a social situation being handled. Naturally, there can be a very wide range of factors which influence the nature of the language used: the social situation, political constraints, the linguistic ability of the participants in the discourse, their attitudes, aims and desires. These factors might indeed involve Jakobson's emotive and phatic functions—but, at the level of second language learning and teaching, the language we are concerned with is largely referential. It *states* ('I am a visitor. I have no money.'); it *shows* ('This is a table; this is a chair.'), which is the deictic, or indicating, kind of language use. And it encompasses the basic range of functions, from agreeing or apologising, through offering, requesting or rejecting, to verifying and wishing.

What referential language in itself does not do is to engage the interlocutors' imaginative faculties. It is transaction-based, socially conditioned, and motivated by a social or personal rationale. Referential language is almost exclusively limited to everyday real-life situational use. As such, it is necessarily the mainstay of basic language use and, consequently, the basis of all second language learning.

Survival language is almost totally referential—unless jokes can come into survival situations. But this they are unlikely to do in the target language. An ability to make a joke already indicates a capacity to move away from the purely referential frame and to use a different range of linguistic, emotional and cultural references, and social attitudes. It indicates that there is for the speaker who makes the joke a *representation*, in a different key, so to speak, of a basic, referentially-enclosed situation.

Representational language opens up, calls upon, stimulates and uses areas of the mind, from imagination to emotion, from pleasure to pain, which referential language does not reach. Where referential language informs, representational language involves.

This distinction is best illustrated in its application to texts as language-learning materials. There has been a fair amount of discussion about affective learning, and clearly the present argument must concern itself with that area of educational experience. But the use of representational materials goes further; rather than seeking consciously to promote affective learning, it almost auto-matically brings about personal interaction between text and reader, between the readers themselves, between teacher and students, above all between the producer and the receiver of the message represented by the text.

Many language-learning materials have begun to take steps towards the use of representational texts, giving a token nod in the direction of imaginative involvement with the use of illustrations or of passages, frequently adapted from novels and stories. Too often, however, this kind of activity has been considered the luxury, or up-market, end of the language-teaching spectrum. It is seen as OK once in a while, suitable for fairly advanced learners or for that ambiguous area, the conversation class. For many teachers, it gets in the way of 'real' language teaching.

What is 'real' language teaching? Certainly the state of play would now cover: communication, with a wide range of functions; grammar, with a greater or lesser emphasis on learning the rules; skills development, according to needs; vocabulary acquisition; and, possibly, a range of social skills such as turn-taking, politeness strategies, and similar forms of interactional awareness.

These are largely mechanical, and measurable, areas of language learning. And they will remain the necessary foundation of learning a language. But imaginative appeal is not restricted to higher levels. Nor should it be considered a luxury.

Language is used for much more than simply conveying infor-mation which is to be received and understood. There is a wide range of discourse whose primary goals go far beyond informative ones. It would be fruitless to try to list such types of discourse, but literature (with a small 'l') can usefully serve as a blanket term to cover the kind of texts we will go on to examine.

What happens when a reader looks at a text should not have to be conditioned in any way by the fact that it is, or is not, a literary text.

What every language textbook teaches is examples or models of usable referential language, which students are encouraged to adopt, follow and manipulate in a given series of contexts or situations, such that their ability to recall and manage these or similar models will be equal to the task of the highest practical test of language use—getting by and making themselves understood in an English-speaking context. Very often, of course, in the institutionalised way of things, real life does not actually enter into the process. The classroom is often the only area where communication in the target language is tried out. Learning achievement is tested by means of some agreed examination procedure whose aims are, more often than not, geared to the learners' requirements in a rather abstract way. The ability to negotiate some communicative and/or grammatical hurdles, to state an opinion or two, to discuss technical matters related to a curriculum and to express themselves at a certain standard in English, gains the student the requisite marks or credits, and fulfils the basic aims of the course to the general satisfaction of all concerned.

In the context of ESL, the situation is not so very different: the strategy is basically one of survival, not necessarily of integration. The ESL learner is given help in preparing to act a role, that of one who lives in an English-speaking environment and who can go through all the basic procedures required of a member of that society.

It is becoming more and more evident, however, that the cultural gap between native speakers and non-native speakers, whether they are learning English as a second language or as a foreign language, is widening rather than narrowing. The language is not functioning as a shared means of expression, but is indeed in many contexts—especially in the larger cities of Great Britain and the United States—a barrier to shared cultural awareness, which forces the non-native speaker back into his or her own culture, and thereby into a kind of ghetto, with a vast series of social and political consequences. A shared language needs shared communication in order to fulfil its function. That communication comes from the individual speaker and is an assertion of the individual, where the retreat into cultural defensiveness is an assertion of the collective.

Most language teachers, in my experience, agree that to get the students talking is both the most difficult thing and the most satisfying thing in the classroom. Clearly, there is a range of ways of doing this which experience has confirmed: pop songs (often, however, with the request that the lyrics be translated), Snoopy cartoons, international TV successes, have become clichés of this kind of up-to-date communication stimuli. In general they work, but it is equally true to say that their use suffers from the absence of a rationale or coherent methodology. So they often end up as the pleasurable content to fill out the last ten minutes or so of a lesson, rather than being properly and fully integrated into the language-learning process. For that very reason, a great many teachers reject them as trivial, mindless entertainment, incapable of making a real contribution to students' learning. Many teachers feel a little guilty about using such materials, feeling caught between serious 'input' and communicative practice, and the accusation of time-wasting. The key question at all times must be: What have the students learned?

What is at issue here boils down to the difference between referential and representational language. The four skills—speaking, listening, reading, writing—are of varying degrees of importance to the second language learner. A learner who requires a basic ability to read, say, medical or technical journals may be perfectly happy with only that ability, although he may occasionally find himself in difficulties speaking. Similarly, an import/export agent may only have to write letters, orders and invoices in English. A student may be perfectly happy merely getting through his examination, without giving any thought to the future usefulness of the language he has been studying. An immigrant in an inner city may only wish to be able to communicate in the most basic terms with social workers, health visitors and the bureaucracy of the area he or she lives in. However, each and every one of them needs an ability which is too often ignored in the learning/teaching nexus: what we might term the fifth skill, *thinking in English*.

Referential language ('This is a table.' 'I am a boy.' 'My name is Federico.' 'Where is the nearest estate agent?') requires very little in the way of thinking. It requires a memory for vocabulary and an ability to manipulate grammatical forms; most native speakers have never given a second thought to such problems as the formation of negatives and interrogatives from an affirmative phrase. The process whereby 'He knew my sister' becomes 'Did he know my sister?' or 'He didn't know my sister' is one that a native speaker does not have to think about, but one which creates often insurmountable problems for the non-native learner.

The learner often loses his communicative impetus simply because he has to devote so much concentration to the mechanical aspects of grammatical manipulation. The content becomes subordinate to the mechanics of the language. The student is thus easily discouraged and demotivated, and communication is lost. Communicative competence, necessarily, is often tested as the ability to overcome these problems. Less importance is frequently given to the significance of what is actually being communicated. When the communication is based on referential language; this is inevitable; talking about the weather, for instance, then becomes a test of an item ('What's the weather like?' 'It's cloudy.').

In normal native-speaker communication, talking about the weather may have a quite different cultural connotation—frequently the communication is phatic rather than informational or deictic. The non-native speaker may justifiably feel left out of the conversational scene, as much for his grammar as for his inability to tune in to the register of the interaction. When, for example, a taxi driver initiates a conversation with, 'It's turned out quite mild,' no specific response is required. In fact, were you to go into details of the weather where you have just come from ('Well, actually, it was snowing in Inverness when I left,' or, 'Actually I find it cold; I've just come back from Nigeria'), it would be more than the conversational starter was intended to elicit and, in politeness terms, would severely alter the rather delicate balance of phatic, time-passing, inconsequential conversation during a taxi ride.

Referential language is, at best, no more than a very basic framework for communicative survival in carefully circumscribed environmental contexts. The primary function of ideational or representational materials is to expand these circumscribed contexts and give as wide a frame of linguistic reference as possible to the basic utterance and the word it employs. The result is that, at whatever level the student studies English (although this will be true in any other language-learning context too), and for whatever purpose—specific, academic, or otherwise—he or she has to *think* about the content of what is being said, heard, read or written, and consequently is more aware of the many forces at play in the producing and receiving of any communicative act.

The more it is developed, the more this awareness leads to an awareness of language as such, and to a consciousness of what is happening during communication; all of which is, I will argue, a fundamental part of the cognitive processes involved in the growth of linguistic fluency. As Halliday (1985/1989:98) confirms: 'Learning is essentially a process of constructing meanings; and the cognitive component in learning is a process of constructing linguistic meanings—semantic systems and semantic structures.' It is an imaginative process, involving cognition and interpretation, rather than a quantifiably scientific process which can be measured in the same terms for every learner. The learner, not unlike the native-speaker infant, develops linguistically at an individual rate of progress. But it would be a mistake to insist too closely on the parallels with the L1 learning process, because the L2 learner is, above all, *fully conscious* of his or her role as a learner, conscious of mistakes (and frequently inhibited by them), conscious that something is happening to his or her capabilities in the learning of the second language. This consciousness should be put to constructive use.

It is my contention that a methodology for the use of representational and ideational materials in language teaching will make use of students' capacities for self-awareness, and lead them to a wider knowledge of the target language and to a greater fluency in it. The approach can be used at all levels (except perhaps that most depressing of all learning thresholds, the pre-beginner). Indeed, the earlier it is used, the better.

2 THE TEACHER AND THE LEARNER

WHAT DOES THE TEACHER NEED IN ORDER TO BE ABLE to approach the use of representational materials in a language-teaching environment? The answer is, perhaps surprisingly, very little. Many language teachers have told me they feel rather inadequate when faced with 'literature', either because they have no 'literary' qualification or because they have not studied literature since their university days. Others leap in enthusiastically because they enjoyed studying literature, because they read a lot, or, because it seems like fun. Each of these approaches—negative and positive—should be treated with caution.

Let us take the enthusiast first. Enthusiasm is always a help in teaching, but it should always be tempered with a clear awareness of students' needs, reactions and responses. None of us wants to turn out like the rather pathetic but (I imagine) pretty familiar figure of the teacher who emotes his or her favourite texts (romantic poetry, very often) to classes whose reaction is bemused or, worse, amused incomprehension; this is 'missionary' work, and it fails to convince.

We are all to some extent missionaries, but our enthusiasm has to be tempered with a professional awareness of *why* we are using the text. It is that *why* which can also furnish the literature-shy teacher with all the basic resources required to tackle the use of literature in language teaching. Lack of experience or of background study will be overcome fairly rapidly by any teacher who wants to overcome them. As long as the text is teachable, and apposite to the class it is intended for, any initial nervousness and hesitation will give way to satisfaction, as the experiment proves its viability.

Dynamic learning and areas of resistance

It is worth making the distinction here between *static and dynamic* learning. Teacher input, to be assimilated and reproduced, invites static, almost mechanical learning. Interaction, learner involvement, inductive learning, all contribute to making the process of learning dynamic.

It is obvious, though immensely important, that a student's active vocabulary, the words he or she can actually produce, is always smaller than his or her passive or receptive vocabulary (the words the student can recognise, infer or guess the meaning of, or simply just assimilate in context). The development of reading competence in a dynamic way implies a growth in these receptive, intuitive, inductive skills.

Representational materials are intended to encourage dynamic learning -learning which involves the student as actively and as personally as possible. The student learns from the surrounding world rather than just from the teacher and the course book. It follows that dynamic learning requires materials which appeal to the learner. This appeal can take many forms: topical relevance, theme, extra-curricular reference, visual impact, humour, emotional impact, etc. Teachers will frequently use a newspaper article in class, finding its topical relevance attractive. Its use can easily be justified in terms of reading skills development, information search, vocabulary enrichment, discussion potential, and so on. But the same teachers may very well shy away from using an imaginative text on the same subject. The teaching aims might be equally justifiable under similar headings to those used to justify the use of the newspaper piece. But the reluctance to use an imaginative text may be distilled down to some fairly clear areas of resistance.

The areas of resistance (or inhibition factors) most commonly found in the language-teaching profession, which work against the use of imaginative, ideational or representational materials, are:

- Literature;
- ignorance of the subject;
- different learning purpose;
- difficulty/complexity
- style
- extracts;
- ambiguity;
- boredom;
- inhibition (teacher and/or student);
- minority taste

These need to be examined one by one.

The institutionalising capital letter in 'Literature' is one of the great inhibition factors which prevents teachers using representational materials in language teaching. This probably goes back to how these teachers were themselves taught Literature at school and university or, if they never studied the subject, to an impression of how daunting the subject is.

This is an understandable reaction. But since we are not talking about Literature courses, many of the standard objections or obstacles fall by the wayside: heavy reading load, reading speed, emphasis on the classics and the canon, the institutionalisation of literature, *having* to read certain texts, studying and analysing literature, critical approaches, appreciation. These may be integral to certain literature courses, but are decidedly not necessary in a course which uses representational, materials as part *of language learning*. With such barriers removed in the minds of both teachers and learners, a whole new range of learning possibilities is opened up.

But there may still be the old question of the teacher's feeling inadequate to the task, a kind of 'Who's afraid of *Who's Afraid of Virginia Woolf?*'

'I'm not a literature person.'
'I don't know anything about literature.'
'I'm not into that sort of thing.'

An astonishing number of teachers in EFL come out with this sort of statement, which effectively imprisons them in the language ghetto, and keeps representational materials as far away from the language classroom as possible. People feel they have to have *read* a literary work before they can use it; or that they have to know about the author, the period, the conventions, the style and what have you, in order to tell the students about them.

Why is teaching *telling?* In the teaching of literature, questions such as teacher-talking time and communicative interaction, which are so carefully thought out in relation to *language* classes, are often simply forgotten. Teacher input takes over.

'Ah, yes,' many a teacher will object, 'but students have got to know about the period, the background, the author.' Indeed. But, as W. H. Auden said, 'A shilling life will give you all the facts.'

The best lessons, in students' terms, are those which they could *not* have got out of some book or other. And why should there be such a concentration on the facts anyway? Does that not bring us right back to Mr Gradgrind in *Hard Times?* 'Facts alone are wanted in life. Plant nothing else, and root out everything else.' An overemphasis on facts in that novel is neatly contrasted with the appeal to the imagination; which brings us right back to the interactive relationship between reader and writer, which is at the heart of all text-based study.

No previous experience of literature as literature is necessary for a teacher to be able to use representational materials in language teaching. And as regards information search with referential materials, the problem of 'not knowing' is easily dealt with because *linguistically* the teacher knows more than the learner (although, in the specialist subject, the learner might know very much more than the language teacher will ever know).

However, the language teacher's inherent 'superiority' is a cheat; and some language teachers feel threatened by their own lack of 'knowledge' (or perhaps only 'experience') with literature. A coach and horses can be driven through almost any interpretation of a text, interpretative strategy or pedagogic process. History can easily be rewritten, turning black into white, and it is a rash L2 teacher who would attempt to lay down the law as regards anything but the most obvious of grammatical rules. And even they were made to be broken, at every level from dialect use to poetic licence.

One of the most conditioning of the many determining factors in the teaching and learning of literature lies in the difference between teachers and students. It is in the nature of things that teachers have usually read more, lived more, experienced more, and worked more on the subject they are teaching. And on this basis, they are generally expected to impart knowledge, to *teach* the students in their charge. The relationship is profoundly, and almost necessarily, imbalanced, unequal; and no amount of pretending to identify with the students will change this. Idealism carries every teacher through phases of closer identification with his or her students, but the institutional role is, finally, the one that counts.

Foreign language students can very rarely have anything like their teacher's awareness of the possibilities of the text being studied at any given time. Guidance, awareness of teaching aims and overall objectives therefore become vitally important. It is quite remarkably, indeed frighteningly, easy for a teacher's own views to be taken as the accepted, the most likely, or the most desirable ones. A great deal of literary criticism is, in fact, scarcely veiled propaganda of this kind.

For a teacher to hitch his or her star to any critical approach or fashion is to run the risk of being seen to be vulnerable when other approaches are discovered. How often students compare their teachers at school with those at university, to the obvious detriment of one side or the other!

Does this mean, then, that a catholic approach is needed, that every possible fashion be covered? Not at all; over eclecticism is just as dangerous as blinkered teacher-centrism. Most teachers would have neither the time nor the inclination anyway to pursue every quiddity of critical fashion as far as the classroom. What we have to keep in mind is the *aim* of our teaching—to help students become better readers of the world they live in. *Not* to become literary critics (that might be the aim of a course in criticism), nor teachers, nor linguists, nor translators, nor historians. Better, more aware readers—a simple, but profound aim.

Terminology is, of course, a problem. But language teachers who use representational materials need very little literary or critical metalanguage to be able to exploit the texts they use. Language teaching itself has become shrouded in terminology in recent years, but there is actually no need to become highly philosophical or deadeningly scientific about the teaching of languages. There has been a growing tendency to create a mystique, a jargon-laden science, out of what is to most of its practitioners a profession. As with any profession, the job can be done well or badly, and most of us would hope that the old slogan holds true: 'Our policy is one of continuous improvement.' Mystique making and sham science are to be avoided like the plague, both with referential and with representational materials.

This represents a basically humanist approach to language learning, and it will be worth bearing in mind Adrian Underhill's immensely useful summary of the common themes in humanistic education:

1. high-level health and well-being;
2. the whole person;
3. the human motivation towards self-realisation
4. change and development
5. education as a life-long process
6. respect for an individual's subjective experience;
7. self-empowerment.

Attention to these themes in the classroom requires an attention to what is often called *process*. Process concerns the way in which the content of a lesson, syllabus or curriculum is taught and learnt from the point of view of the learner, and how that content can become directly relevant to the lives of the learners. Process focuses on the immediate subjective reality of the individuals in a learning group, and is concerned with how participants relate to themselves and each other in order to carry out the task. Whatever contributes to the ambient learning atmosphere, including the attitudes, values and awareness of the teacher and of the learners, is part of the process.

(UNDERHILL 1989:261)

It should be clear that the present approach shares much of this concern with *process*, and with the consequent focus on subjectivity and the learner. The teacher, however, must always have learning objectives in mind for any teaching initiative.

If teachers have clear teaching aims in mind, many of their daunting, institutional, atavistic fears can be dispelled, and the literature enjoyed *for itself,* without any need for apology, intrusion in the process of student interaction with the text or, deadliest of all, standing in front of the text in order to explain or 'explicate' it.

If the text is interesting, rewarding and stimulating to you, the teacher, you should probably be able to find its teachable qualities and start working with it in class from there. Never feel you have something to apologise for, either to the students for using 'litera-ture', or—because of the 'I-haven't-actually-read-George-Eliot' syndrome—to some imaginary all-knowing, widely-read person of letters.

Similarly, but conversely, there is the risk of overkill; reading a new novel in bed, you find a wonderful passage and just have to take it into class the next day. Very few texts, teachers or classes merit this. Take it coolly and find objectively why the text is worth using, and you will get a lot more out of it.

There is no point in trying to pretend that something is great literature either; it falls to remarkably few critics to change the canon. So don't over-react, oversell or overvalue: let the text speak for itself. The students will soon tell you what they think of it and, at the end of the day, it is what they say and how they say it that matters.

'Never apologise, never explain,' the old maxim goes. Justifica-tion beyond students' language-learning development is not neces-sary, and literature as a specialised subject is only a question of intensity and focus.

Scales and contexts of learning

The learning purpose is different in language teaching: to paraphrase Widdowson, not only language use is conditioned by learning purpose, but also teaching strategy. It should be obvious that teaching strategies for the use of representational materials will be considerably different from teaching strategies for literature courses.

We can identify *scales of learning* here, which must be closely related to *contexts of learning*. Frequently, apart from of course the situational context of a learning institution in (probably) a country other than that of the target language, *text is context* in using representational materials. The assimilation or accommodation of what is learnt depends very much on the personal context in which the learner interprets the educational experience. Teachers have to beware of leaving what is learnt completely in the realm of the unpredictable.

On our scales of learning, we may find:

- participation
- rejection
- assimilation
- observation

Participation happens in class and involves student/teacher interaction, student/student interaction, and student/text interaction. The second and, more often, the third of these can become *extended participation* outside class time.

Rejection can happen at any time. But it is not necessarily to be considered as negative. If a student rejects a learning mode or a text, it is probably due either to psychological factors or to a wrong choice on the part of the teacher, in which case, a problem situation has to be remedied. If, however, rejection is an active reaction to the materials presented, the teacher should encourage a move on the student's part from intuitive to more considered rejection, building on the student's affective response, and allowing scope for discussion and possible interaction with other students. This is rejection shaped into controversy, rather than left as rejection out of hand. Learning occurs when the student has to justify the original rejection, and the next two stages may follow, just as they would have done had the text not been rejected.

Assimilation at the cognitive level can involve simple recognition, comprehension, decoding and understanding. That is, a series of outside strategies are brought to bear on the text, with more or less help from the teacher or other students, such that the student is enabled to assimilate either what the teacher has directed learner interest towards, or what he or she personally and individually is attracted by. This is still a fairly subjective stage of learning.

Observation takes the process a little further. For, both during and after the processes of rejection or assimilation, students will have to take into account peer reaction and response. Observing this, the individual student has to decide whether to align him- or herself with the stated viewpoints of colleagues. Observation encourages the kind of reflection which can lead to the taking up of positions, or at least to the statement of opinions. Outside and inside factors are thus brought to bear on the learning process.

With representational materials, the learning process goes on well beyond the actual didactic moment. Comprehension is a stimulus rather than an end in itself; so what happens in the learner's consciousness, after a level of understanding of the text has been reached, becomes a highly significant part of the learning experience. Meaning-focused activity in class becomes, potentially, the starting-point for reflection and cross-reference, as the learner's memory stores the cultural, ideational and linguistic throughput for further consideration, application and recycling. Add to this the possible 'time-bomb' effect of a text's becoming significant, relevant or in some other way useful, after a period 'in cold storage' subsequent to the original learner/text encounter.

Imaginative transfer from what has been comprehended into something which can be referred to, brought back into discussion at a later date (as in, 'Do you remember that text we read about the plums in the icebox?') occurs as a longer-term learning benefit from the use of representational materials.

When a student recalls and recycles a text that he or she has already read in a second, later context, this imaginative cross-reference is, I suggest, a sign that language learning has moved beyond the merely referential, and that a declarative framework of representational reference is being built up. The teacher, in encouraging such continual cross-reference, is in effect reinforcing the representational content of the syllabus and course. This is one of the empirical ways by which we can move some way towards the viability of a representational syllabus. It also confirms that an absence of specific learning targets does not necessarily imply the absence of learning or of a viable learning structure.

Questions of difficulty and complexity are relative. Accessibility must always be the key-note, and this is examined on pages ??-??. The suitability of the text to the learners' needs is also vital to the successful use of representational materials. The fact that representational texts are significantly more complex, both in linguistic and content terms, may be adduced here. As Gunther Kress puts it, 'all texts are marked by the presence of multiplicity of discourse,' (Kress, 1988:136). But language teachers are not textual analysts, and it will very rarely be necessary to go into intertextual relations, 'fusions of discourse' or similarly technical areas, if the texts used are chosen with language-teaching viability as the prime criterion.

Similarly, style can be a highly complex area of analysis. It is notoriously one of the most ambiguous concepts in literary study, and one of the most difficult to define (see Leech and Short, 1981). It can be summed up for our purposes as the fingerprinting of a text, which emerges from such components as lexis, syntax, cohesion, phonology, graphology, register, genre and other more subjective criteria. But this need only concern the language teacher and learner at a fairly superficial level.

It is worth remembering, however, that all expression has style of some kind or another. 'Absence of style' is, in its way, a kind of style. But stylistic variants rarely actually change the meaning, especially in a short text of the kind language teachers are most likely to be working with.

Widdowson's concern with 'deviance' from grammatical rules (1986:15ff etc.) has been interpreted unduly negatively. Rules, as the saying goes, were made to be broken. I prefer to use the idea of 'variant' forms in representational language, both to get away from any negative connotations which 'deviant/deviance' may have and to acknowledge the acceptability of the variants from grammatical or lexical norms which such language shows. Students can usefully be encouraged to reflect on what they themselves might have written, in order the better to comprehend the variant lexical or syntactical choices an author has made.

Constraints of time and curriculum objectives dictate that, in general, only brief representational texts can be used in class time. It can be objected that these misrepresent the complete text from which they are extrapolated (see Chapter 6), but there cannot really be serious didactic objections to the use of extracts as such. Extensive reading, possibly motivated by the reading of attractive extracts, is a sign of success in the use of imaginative materials. Ambiguity in texts is to be enjoyed, as is shown in Chapter 8. Boredom will only set in, in teachers and students, when there is nothing more that the participants can get from the text.

Some texts are more exploitable than others; frequently, especially early on in language learning, it is advisable to use representational material for only one short, sharp, effective purpose. To go any more deeply into the text might prove daunting and demotivating. Boredom in language learning is almost always caused by lack of motivation.

If a teacher is inhibited about bringing affective aspects into the language classroom, there is something a little bit wrong. There is no need to become too personal, either as regards yourself or in inviting student participation. In some cultures, discussion, especially of a personal nature, is anathema in an educational context— Japan is a case in point. But personal matters can quite easily be kept at arm's length without sacrificing spontaneity, expression of opinion, reactions and responses. How much the teacher or student can introduce personal factors into the classroom must be judged according to local situations, customs and needs. Inhibition, at any level of language learning, can be a considerable impediment—psychological or social—to successful educational achievement.

Finally, yes, Literature may be a minority interest, but literature is not. The imagination is open to all, and only attempts to circumscribe the imagination can hive off certain kinds of imaginative production into minority-taste areas. Likes and dislikes certainly have to be taken into account, and 'I don't like reading' is perhaps the most serious area of resistance of all. Little by little, the enthusiastic teacher has to try to break down this kind of resistance. It certainly will not disappear of its own volition, so it is up to the teacher, and the texts, to change the reluctant reader's attitude.

3 STUDENTS AND READING

IT IS TOO EASY TO SAY, 'OUR STUDENTS DON'T READ'. IN fact, they have never been accustomed to reading, or, more importantly, to reading *for pleasure;* they have never been educated or stimulated into the habit of reading, a habit which, if acquired when young, will give lasting pleasure through life.

So, our complaint that students don't read implies a lot more than that they don't want to read. They don't know *how* to read properly, *why* they should read at all, *what* reading can give them. All these things are called into question when we face the question of reading in a computer-dominated world.

To read properly, fully, with a deep and satisfying understanding of what a writer is saying, is not an easily acquired ability, since it involves a whole series of skills and capacities which go very far beyond the traditional pupil's concept of reading. 'To read = to study' for a great many students. So, the reading that they do is limited in scope and direction: it takes them as far as an examination, and very often no further.

This examination-oriented mentality on the part of the student is, in great measure, the result of generations of teachers feeling insecure in themselves, and overcompensating for unmerited feelings of inadequacy by pushing students single-mindedly towards examinations. And certainly we cannot blame the conscientious teacher, who naturally wants to see as many students as possible getting good results in their examinations. But, at a certain point in this process, and it is a point fairly early on in the process itself, the true value of education, the idea of 'education for life' can all too easily be forgotten, as the examination or the ministerial programme take over. How often teachers have found themselves teaching things they would prefer not to teach, while not being able to teach the things they would enjoy teaching, just because the prescribed syllabus has to be closely followed.

It is in reading that this lost space can be recovered: it is a space for the exercise of mental energy; it is a space for creativity; it is a space where the personal elements of interaction, involvement, concern, and personality can all be accommodated. For too long they have been left outside the classroom door when the teacher has entered the room.

In practical terms, some people might want to argue, is it not better for the students to work with what they want to, rather than for teachers to insist on instilling old forms into them?

The answer to that question is a complex one indeed. For, certainly, teachers must always be in the vanguard of modern methodologies and techniques. And no-one would deny the enormous value of such innovations as the computer and video in classroom teaching. But what we are talking about is the minds of our students, the cultural, aesthetic, social and philosophical values that will make them better citizens of the world. And here it is very difficult to draw the line between indoctrination on the one hand, and the development of free expression, individual critical and responsive capacities—in short, the acquiring of personal criteria of taste and sensibility—on the other.

The most profoundly useful sphere of operation for computer technology in educational terms will remain the fields of mathematics and science, although significant steps are being made in the field of CALL (Computer Assisted Language Learning). What we have not yet overcome, or, at least, what we have not yet convinced our students of, is the very important fact that computers only think as much or as little as they have been programmed to think. The human mind is not substituted by the computer (hence the fact that it is called, in English, 'artificial intelligence'); this is the crux of the problem. For, at the present time, there are too many possibilities of 'artificial intelligence' making life easy for us—for instance, we no longer have to do the kind of calculations that only a generation ago were commonplace.

The world has shrunk, but with it there is also the danger of laziness entering into our thinking processes; and our students' minds can shrink too, as a consequence. When the computer can do our thinking for us, or television can do our imagining for us, it is very easy for us to let these capacities lapse in ourselves.

It is clear that a film of, for example, *The Dead* or *The Garden of the Finzi-Continis* or *A Room with a View,* is more immediately accessible to an audience than the book upon which it was based. But the film must be considered as a stimulus to reading, rather than as a substitute for it—this argument has gone on since the cinema was invented. So, is that all that can be said? Do we try to make our students read Joyce, Bassani, and Forster, and hope that a few of them will prefer the original words to the second-hand images? That would be a coward's way out.

The crisis of literature as a subject, in effect, represents only a small part of a universal cultural crisis because, although man is, as Aristotle said, a being of the word, it is not at all beyond the bounds of possibility that the next age will not express itself in words. Not by chance many of the greatest writers of our time are moving closer and closer to silence—the late Samuel Beckett is the most significant example.

A lot of past literature has passed into the realms of specialization. Many of the greatest literary figures of the Western world are now 'studied' rather than read; that is, students and academics work on them, write about them, prepare themselves for examinations on them, dissect them, deconstruct them, analyse them—going so far beyond merely *reading* them that they seem to do anything *except* actually read them—which was, after all, what the writer originally intended for the work.

I do not want to suggest that there is not a place for the academic study of literature—quite the contrary! But, in practical terms, I do want to suggest that it is not necessary for the text to be weighed down with study, nor is it totally unacademic to make *le plaisir du texte* part of students' regular classroom experience.

What we are in fact contrasting is the acceptance of instant satisfactions in modern culture, as opposed to lasting satisfactions. It is in the nature of consumer society, and in the nature of media production (television, records, fashion, books) that tastes change rapidly, that the market continually produces new artefacts, and that long-term appreciation of a cultural phenomenon is lessened. Market value becomes fashion value, which becomes instant value: small wonder that much of literature is thus considered old-fashioned, irrelevant and, dare we say it, boring.

We have to remember that there is, and always must be, a great gap between reading on the one hand, and teaching and learning Literature on the other. What I am saying here does not really regard the latter activities which are the deeply involved subject of a great deal of research and which present their own range of problems and potential solutions. Rather, my concern is for the kind of reading that *every* student can do, and that, unfortunately, many are never encouraged to do. There is usually no shortage of good materials on the market for reading, in the students' own language as well as in the other languages studied in school curricula. What is lacking, then? Because most of us would admit that something is wrong, although we would not necessarily be able to put our finger on precisely what it is.

I think the root of the whole problem of reading in the context of the school can be traced to one long-standing educational obsession, and that is the obsession with the *whole* text. The tendency is to have less faith in the extract, the representative passage which, if very carefully chosen, can stimulate students' interest more than any long stretch of intensive reading. However, sensitive text selection, a theme-based approach, and a development of interactional potentialities of texts can offer a valid and practical solution to the problem.

Then again, there are those students who *do* read, enthusiastically and regularly, in the language they are learning. The motivations for their enthusiasm may be:

- cultural (out of interest, for personal or study reasons)
- social (elitism; one-upmanship, 'Have you read...?')
- educational (EAP; education for life)
- selfish (for pleasure, enjoyment, entertainment—usually anathema in a learning context!)

Such keenness is not as widespread as it might be—and is usually the result of self-motivation rather than of carefully planned and successful teaching. Self-motivation should not be undervalued in this kind of context.

Much of the literature of the past can very usefully be recovered as reading material for the present generation: the difficulty does not lie in the literature, but with the methods and techniques used to present it to the students. *Accessibility* must always be the keynote. And to render a text accessible does not mean trivialising the text or compromising it. Simply, it means finding the correct and apposite point of entry for present-day students into texts which are not at first sight directly relevant or interesting to them. This involves an immensely careful process of selection; not, we must stress, a process of censoring, doctoring or indoctrination, but a careful study of what the text is for, why it was written, and its points of validity to present-day circumstances.

Students enjoy finding out how things work—this can be one of the first areas of enjoyment, as they find out how a text works. Learning to read has always implied recognising letters, then forming words, then putting these words together, and extending the process to longer pieces of writing. But in general, our students are not actually taught how to read a passage to see how it is constructed; nor how to find out quickly the gist of a text, how to bring out information from what they are reading. All these techniques have been applied to reading texts specific to foreign language learning, but little of this technical help has been brought to bear on the wider range of reading that students should be engaged in.

No magic or trickery, no transformations or concessions are needed, no superficial 'sugaring of the pill' is necessary—just dedicated understanding of the exigencies of text and student, and, above all, of communication. This is communication between text and teacher, between teacher and student, between student and student, between student and self, but, above all—and this is the aim of the whole enterprise—between student and text, and thus between receiver and producer, reader and writer. This is the relationship that must be at the heart of all reading, and the basis of all education in reading.

The world we live in is not simply made up of 'facts', despite the statisticians' attempts to dominate our lives: man cannot live by bread alone, or by facts alone, or by figures and diagrams. There is and always must be a life of the mind. When we, as teachers, say that our students do not have a life of the mind, we are guilty of not appreciating what goes on in their minds, and of not trying to connect with it. We can learn from them, as they can from us; texts, and the discussion of them, can function as the intermediary between us, as between past and present, our generation and their generation.

When we talk about reading, we do not only mean texts, verbal or non-verbal as they may be. Reading, in any age, also means reading the world, attempting to interpret, to come to terms with, to assimilate, perhaps even one day to understand what surrounds us, in order that we be better equipped to live in the world. And just as the world must constantly interest, fascinate and surprise us, so our reading must stimulate, provoke, irritate and *teach* us. Thus we expand our horizons, we compare and contrast our experiences, we react and respond outside the classroom, much as we learned to do inside the classroom.

In short, by reading the world, we help ourselves and our students to live better in the world. If we can convince students that there are structures of feeling in the world (the phrase was coined by Raymond Williams and is supremely valid in this context), we will have shown them that reading develops understanding, influences feelings, helps us see and experience our world better. It can be the most complete and therefore the most satisfying of learning and educational experiences. Deeper satisfactions than instantly available ones can convince teachers and students alike that reading is not a lost cause, not a tedious chore, but a vital part of our progress as human beings. As we move beyond the initial flirtatious enthusiasm for computers, our schools will find the equilibrium again, and reading, with the full use of representational materials in all subjects and at all levels, will assume its rightful place in the education of all learners.

Christopher Brumfit (1985:116) posits four factors which have to be taken into account as readers move towards literature: a language minimum, cultural reference, literary convention, and intellectual demands. But he stresses the difference between the use of representational materials and the development of 'literary competence'—so, worries about literary conventions can be kept to a minimum in the present context. And intellectual demands have to be gauged in any reading context—the teacher can only take his or her students so far down the intellectual pathways of literature.

'Intellectual' is frequently adduced as a negative term. Indeed, some language teachers' attitude to literature is that it is off-puttingly intellectual. In the present context, we are trying to encourage students to read, so, although we are not wanting to sugar the pill, I feel that intellectualism is best left out of the argument, particularly at lower levels of language ability (although, clearly, language competence does not necessarily reflect intellectual ability). Readers who wish to reach higher intellectual levels will simply have a further motivation for their reading, both in their own language and in the language they are learning.

One cannot go very far down this road without mentioning Krashen and his 'input hypothesis'. Certainly, in an ideal world, the notion that the more students read, the more they will want to read, would be delightful. In the real world, it does not work like that. Input has to be carefully selected and monitored (as Krashen clearly recognises), and what works well with one class might not work with another at the same level. Different countries, cultures and learning situations require different approaches and solutions: what works in Miami might mystify in Malawi, and Bulgarians might baulk at what Bolivians enjoy.

For that reason, no theory of reading, of input or of the value of representational materials will ever be watertight and applicable to every situation. Theory must always be tested and tempered by practice; and one teacher's practice might be another teacher's poison.

Theoreticians and those who would give practical instructions can realistically hope only to encourage teachers to experiment with new ideas, to be prepared to run a few (controlled) risks, to cultivate a more intellectually interactive relationship with their students. Teacher development is largely a question of building up teacher confidence, in terms of language, culture and professional didactic abilities.

Many teachers are understandably sceptical of new fashions, techniques, -isms and -ologies. Experience tells us there is nothing new under the sun—just different ways of looking at things. A representational approach will not overturn any long-standing theories. But it might enrich them, and give teachers and learners something more satisfying to get their teeth into.

Preparing the students

First of all, it is not necessary to treat the use of representational materials as something strange or new; it's no big thing from that point of view. What it *is* necessary to stress is the flexibility and openness of the reading experience, the possibility of individual reaction and response.

If students are introduced to representational materials very early on in the language-learning process, (say after six or seven lessons—even for beginners, when texts like those on pages **77-78** can be introduced), a representational component can be built into *any* language course. A new text or two every week or, at the most, every ten days will give students on-going exposure to the worlds of the imagination and of curiosity and discovery.

This holds good for courses of all kinds: middle-school students, computer programmers, doctors, hotel receptionists, air crews, mechanical engineers, agricultural experts, teachers, nuclear physicists, political scientists, electricians, dentists, prisoners, immigrant housewives, soldiers, secretaries, export managers, bankers—all these, and hundreds of other kinds of language learn-ers, have an imagination and enjoy using it.

With regular use, representational materials will become an enjoyable and indispensable part of language learning. Students will be more highly motivated, and will look forward to the unpre-dictable nature of the materials—which usually contrast with the fairly predictable material in textbooks, largely referential in their content and application.

The question inevitably arises as to whether to use a book or photocopies of materials, whether to have students buy a represen-tational materials book or have the school or institution acquire class sets.

In practice, most teachers simply do not have the time to seek out, prepare and collect sufficient quantities of representational materials. Naturally, such collections are to be encouraged, and a representational materials library should be just as much part of a good school's resources as the picture library, the newspaper cuttings collection, the song cassettes, the self-access centre, and so on.

Books of representational materials are becoming more numer-ous. Almost every publisher's catalogue now boasts one or two, although these are often described as being for intermediate to advanced students. This label is often very necessary, but can, equally, be misleading and restrictive: where the materials in the book are grouped together thematically, the levels of single texts may not be so restricted, although older texts and some complete units might be accessible only to more advanced learners. Some books attempt some grading of accessibility levels within units and this can help the teacher considerably, although such grading should in no way be taken as definitive, restrictive or limiting: the teacher must always make the final decision as to what the class will be able to handle and how to present it successfully.

Photocopying is the bane of authors' and publishers' lives. In my own experience, students are not particularly happy with photocopied materials either. The learner has to collect, organise, and file them; and often just does not want to, or have time to make that effort. Obviously, all of us use photocopied materials from time to time—for one-off lessons, because we have just found a good text, or because a book we want is not available locally. But photocopying is not to be encouraged, for methodological as well as for legal copyright reasons.

It is useful for students to be able to look back at materials they have handled in class, both for their own enjoyment and for their longer-term educational benefit as their range of reading reference expands. This also means that they are encouraged to explore other texts which might not have been read in class but which are grouped together, in a unit of a book, with materials already familiar to the student.

Individual further reading, using single texts as a jumping-off point, can best be encouraged if students have (or have access to) a book of representational materials. I have frequently seen it happen that, after using photocopies for three or four single lessons, students actually ask where they can buy or consult the book the texts were taken from. Part of the discovery of the pleasure of reading must come from the book being read: content, look, feel, and (of course) price can all encourage students to start building up a library of books they are happy to own.

Class sets are invaluable, and failure to invest in them is a false economy. Ten or twenty copies of two or three carefully chosen books—with, if possible, one or two copies of the teacher's book and the cassette(s) (if available)—provide a constant resource, which might lead to the installation of a lending library of imaginative reading materials: from readers, to short stories and plays, to complete novels in English.

The development of students' extensive reading is one of the most important concomitant advantages in the regular class-time use of representational materials. Students are encouraged to move from short texts to slightly longer ones—to read on, as they find titles, genres, subjects or authors they enjoy—and they develop, as a result, a degree of reader autonomy which takes them far beyond the imaginative language-learning benefit of the original classroom encounter with representational materials.

4 LEARNING OBJECTIVES

Course and content

HOW MUCH IMAGINATIVE REPRESENTATIONAL MATERIAL can be built into a language course? The question is rather like asking, 'How long is a piece of string?' If I were to recommend that some sort of representational language be used in every language lesson, it might be argued that I was overstating the case and over-burdening the teacher with a search for appropriate materials. However, the answer to the initial question has to be, 'As much as possible.' It is an attitude of mind on the part of the teacher as well as a methodological decision. A great many highly reputable language schools all over the world still only tolerate the imaginative teacher's occasional use of representational materials as something of an indulgence, something rather outside the 'real' language teaching that is the school's *raison d'etre*. The Director of Studies who says, 'We don't teach literature,' or, worse, 'We don't use that kind of thing,' is guilty of the restrictive schematisation of language learning, which is dangerously close to the 'follow the coursebook' mentality so often prevalent among unadventurous teachers.

Several years ago, Roland Barthes proclaimed 'the death of the author'—and went on to live handsomely on his author's royalties from that text for several years! If I here attempt to announce 'the death of the coursebook', it is with a similarly two-sided axe that I commit the murderous act. Obviously, coursebooks will be ever with us, but a little reflection on how necessary or unnecessary they are would be salutary.

Coursebooks can be the best way of stifling student learning. The teacher who follows any coursebook slavishly will inevitably bore him- or herself as well as the students. And 'getting through the book by the end of the course'—the excuse used by thousands of teachers for not departing from the coursebook—is one of the most counterproductive and openly anti-learning attitudes it is possible to find. The showing of videos of popular films, drama work, folk-song groups, library use—and other such activities involving representational materials, learner interaction, and learner involvement with the materials—are generally seen, in this way of thinking, as extra-curricular activities. Some classroom spin-off may be allowed, if not actively encouraged.

It has to be admitted, however, that the cause of representational materials has not been helped by a kind of over-idealistic humanistic approach, which can lead to arbitrary and undisciplined programmes based on the teacher's likes and whims, with insufficient regard for students' needs and course objectives. This individualistic approach can do more harm than good, although students might *think* they are enjoying themselves. Class time is always limited, and often costs the paying customer a lot, so it has to be used as constructively as possible, with self-indulgence cut to a minimum. This concern is, quite justifiably, at the root of a conscientious Director of Studies' worries.

However, if representational materials are systematically prepared, collected, and made available to teachers, coursebook work can be backed up, confirmed, and enriched in a regular, methodical, and controlled way. Most schools have a resource library or materials stock, but class sets of published materials are often kept only as a token nod in the direction of imaginative involvement, and are not used systematically throughout the courses being taught.

A newspaper cuttings stock, or song sheets, are steps in the right direction. Close and careful integration is required with materials such as graded readers, theme-based materials, extensive reading materials, and extra-curricular language development and improvement activities. A system of cross-reference covering the entire range of materials available at every language-learning level is vital. And teachers, in induction or in-service courses, should be actively encouraged to familiarise themselves with, experiment with, comment on, and add to this range of materials. Too often, teachers work within a limited range of outside materials, perhaps for fear of not completing the course-=book, perhaps simply because of lack of familiarity with the complete range of materials available, and/or lack of encouragement.

A very short in-service course on the use of representational materials with students from beginner to advanced levels— including ESP students—can, in my own experience, radically affect a school's teaching. 'I never realised,' 'I thought it would be difficult,' or 'It's good; the students will love it' are among the most common reactions. Teacher unfamiliarity with representational materials and their potential is just as much a drawback to their more widespread use as the teacher inhibition discussed earlier. And unfamiliarity breeds lack of confidence.

What, then, should teachers be encouraged to do? At in-service courses for various governments—at primary, secondary, and

tertiary levels—and for the leading language-teaching organisa-
tions such as the British Council and International House, I have
found that *simplicity* is the most attractive quality to teachers
unused to representational materials. There is an element here of
demystification, but no sugaring of the pill is actually necessary.

As has already been said, the principal question about which
sceptical teachers, school heads or Directors of Studies need to be
convinced is 'teaching pay-off': what students actually learn as a
result of using representational materials. As we have seen, this
can be measured in various ways:

- language learning;
- receptivity;
- linguistic confidence;
- related world knowledge;
- language description/awareness;
- personal satisfaction
- language practice;
- cultural awareness;
- memory;
- linguistic or aesthetic curiosity;
- active involvement;
- critical evaluation;
- classroom interaction;
- grammatical, structural, or functional reinforcement;
- post-lesson stimuli;
- production;
- information;
- enthusiasm;
- constructive enjoyment.

It often surprises teachers that there can be so many ways of
looking at 'pay-off'. Genuine learning achievement goes far beyond

mastery of functions and grammatical rules, and the fact that many of the pay-off factors listed above are clearly subjective is a vital part of the balance between affective and objective learning which is itself so fundamental to language acquisition.

Language development and language awareness

Many teachers, while working happily at an affective level in inter-personal relationships within the classroom, are wary of risking the introduction of affective elements in open discussion. This is part of the inhibition factor we noticed earlier. But it will be clear by now that of all these possible pay-off factors, a majority do involve some affective elements. In the people business, of which language teaching is an inevitable part, subjectivity cannot be avoided. And just as objectivity is essential in the design and operation of language tests, so the role of subjectivity and individual affective involvement has to be considered as an essential part, not only of linguistic, but also of all educational development.

Talking about what we are learning and teaching is coming to be recognised as a vital part of the process of language learning: it implies a move from direct participation in a learning activity to the objective consideration of the results or usefulness of that activity. 'What will the student learn?' is a question every teacher should ask before embarking on the use of any representational material. The answers may be precise and concrete—in linguistic, cultural, or aesthetic terms—or they may be more abstract—learning *about* something rather than merely learning it. Whatever the teacher's stated or implicit learning objective, it may very well not coincide at all with what the *learner* thinks he or she has learned. 'What have I learned?' may have immediate answers; or it may have long-term answers, imprecise intuitions, a 'nothing' which later turns out as 'something'.

There are occasions, more often at the referential level or in terms of language awareness and description, when it is necessary for the learner and teacher to know and share the learning objectives. However, as soon as the interpretation spectrum opens up, the level of benefit to each learner of what is being studied is only measurable at a personal level. It is therefore very often not quantifiable-although it might be observable, in terms of participation, interaction in group dynamics, linguistic, cultural or world awareness, and any of several affective factors.

Does the use of representational materials help language students pass purely language exams? I would not have written this book if I thought it did not, but the question is a legitimate one. What has to be emphasised here is that 'purely language exams', if they are testing mechanical knowledge of rules, are almost irrelevant to any constructive learning context. Knowledge of use and usage, awareness of L 1 as well as competence in L2, the ability to apply language learning to a range of practical, cultural and social contexts, are all vital elements in the overall linguistic development of any learner.

Language development and cultural awareness go hand in hand. Language is a system of signs and references; the references may be no more than cultural quiddities, but are none the less beyond the referential limitations of language use. I am indebted to Guy Aston for the following example: 'The English put bread and butter and buttered toast on their tea and breakfast tables, not toast and butter and buttered bread, notwithstanding the fact that the latter are grammatically well-formed and situationally appropriate.' (Aston, 1991) This is an arbitrary cultural convention, and one which only familiarity will help the learner to overcome—always assuming the learner *does* want to overcome his or her lack of knowledge of English breakfast conventions!

Many questions are begged here, in fact. At the most trivial level, one could object that learners who do not eat breakfast, those with a high cholesterol level, or those who simply grunt at breakfast, need never get involved in such cultural minutiae. The example is a fairly extreme one, though useful. For it shows us the difficulty teachers will always find in illuminating what native speakers take for granted. Illumination can only be achieved through exemplification or experience.

A referential means of illuminating breakfast language use might involve a situational dialogue, or series of dialogues, a vocabulary list, perhaps a role-play or other reinforcement activity. This would be an enabling exercise inasmuch as the learner would now know the basic mechanics of how to cope with breakfast in England. But what breakfast? Breakfast in general is not breakfast in particular, as any student who has stayed with two different English families will confirm. A whole series of personal, family, class, regional, social, and even socio-political factors can under-mine even the best learner's efforts to cope with an English break-fast. And the pitfalls go far beyond the potential solecism of asking for a piece of buttered bread. The following texts are revealing, and confirm—if confirmation were needed—Saussure's much-quoted observation, 'Language is a social fact,' expanded by Halliday in his equally important statement (1978:1), 'Language is a product of the social process.'

~

Anything interesting in *The Times*?

Don't be silly, Charles.

Claude pinched the last slice of thin bread-and-butter, and Eustace poured himself out a cup of tea.

Next morning he rang me up on the phone just after I'd got the bacon and eggs into my system—the one moment of the day, in short, when a chappie wishes to muse on life absolutely undisturbed.

I met my uncle at breakfast. We said nothing that was at all important. He seemed to find it most impossible to talk to me. The Sunday papers arrived, and I looked at them with apprehension.

On the table, the hosts of breakfast were marshalled into two opposing forces, and a Miss Emery from either end commanded each. The toast, eggs, bacon, and marmalade had declared for Miss Dora; but the tea-pot and its vassals, the cruet and the honeycomb—beautifully bleeding in flowered dish—were for Miss Emery to a man. The loaf, sitting opposite Roger, remained unabashedly neutral. Roger looked from one Miss Emery to the other.

Kidneys were in his mind as he moved about the kitchen softly, righting her breakfast things on the humpy tray.

Adam ate some breakfast. No kipper, he reflected, is ever as good as it smells.

'Oh, never mind about breakfast for me,' interposed sponge. 'I'll have some tea or coffee and chops, or boiled ham and eggs, or whatever's going, in my bedroom,' said he, 'so never mind altering your hour for me.'

Haines came down to breakfast to find Jules at an oak table in the morning-room, porridge and kippers set out before him on a hot-plate. There was as yet no sign for Bessy.

'Ludlow, take away this toast. It's burnt.'

~

This gives a wide range of breakfast tastes, and a range of fairly clear cultural deductions could be drawn from it. But there is no mention of fruit juice and cornflakes, or of those who dash out without breakfast, or of muesli or the *Morning Star*.

What this breakfast selection does show us is that what happens at breakfast goes far beyond any referential description of the meal and the circumstances surrounding it. If students were to be presented with these brief snapshots in order to find out something about the English breakfast, what would they discover? And what cognitive processes would be involved?

The process would be deductive and cumulative, in that information has to be drawn out of the single texts and put together with information from the others. What is eaten—from bread-and-butter to kippers or kidneys—and the facts that a newspaper might be read or that toast should not be burnt; these are concrete. The rest is implicit, covering a range of personal feelings, (un)communicative relationships, and ideas of social context and setting. Students have to go through a process of negotiation with the texts (and possibly with each other) in order to interpret—each according to experience, presuppositions, background knowledge, and external guidance (from the teacher)—and to reach some conclusions.

The process involves affective and cognitive convergence—a movement towards shared understanding. But where this process often leads to the creation of meaning (in an information-gap context, for instance), here the meaning or conclusions arrived at are necessarily open rather than closed; there is not one single 'answer' or 'meaning', but an opening-up of cultural, social and human horizons. This opening-up is usually a second stage in text study in a language-learning context. The first stage necessarily involves understanding: the process of orientation, information search and context assimilation, which then permits the reader to go on to the later, more subjective stages of interpretation, reflection and evaluation.

In this particular case, the context is given, and the reader does not have to work out that the texts are all to do with breakfast (although students could do so without too much difficulty—but not giving this preliminary information would create a kind of deductive puzzle of the texts rather than a culturally motivating exercise). The teacher provides the context, and guides the students to what can be discovered. 'What people have for breakfast/think of at breakfast' might be the overall theme. Reformulated as a lead-in question, that title stimulates a search for information.

Once the information has been gathered, orally or written in columns, what then? This is the moment for the jump from referential to representational. Because, now, intuitive and social factors come into play. If the teacher asks, 'What can you tell about the people having breakfast?', a whole range of interpretative possibilities opens up. What will emerge from the exercise will depend not so much upon the texts themselves as upon what the readers bring to the texts: cultural awareness, sensitivity to point of view, ideas of social class, sense of humour, and so on, must all play a part in this interaction between text and reader.

The result might only be the discovery of new vocabulary, like 'kidney' or 'kipper'; at a slightly higher level, a reinforcement of ideas about how strange the English are; where interaction really takes off, there is a lot of mileage in imagining contexts and characters, situations and circumstances, and in thinking about the tone of the text, the affective context of the moment.

There are no right or wrong answers here: what the individual reader can tell about the couple's relationship from the words 'righting her breakfast things on the humpy tray' is entirely a matter of personal reaction and response. And that reaction can be anything from 'don't care' (in which case the texts have lost their motivating force) to an analysis of a moment in a marriage.

Subjective response is inevitable, and is to be encouraged. Humour is an area worth experimenting with: the first snippet can lead to an identification of the kind of couple speaking (students will almost always say they are 'old') and what kind of communication there is between them. One of my own personal yardsticks of success with representational materials is how much students remember and recycle because the situation has appealed to them or struck a chord. There is a strange satisfaction in overhearing 'Don't be silly, Charles,' recycled in student-student conversations, far removed from the original context.

5 MATERIALS

Non-verbal materials

WHEN LEARNING A LANGUAGE, WORDS AND TEXTS ARE fundamental tools. It is therefore salutary to remember at the outset that representational materials do not necessarily have to be verbal, although the responses they are intended to stimulate in the learner will, almost certainly, involve words in a spoken or written form.

A picture has been said to be something between a thing and a thought. Any kind of illustration or work of visual art—photograph, cartoon, painting, drawing, statue, even a building—is in some way a statement of its creator's intentions. And, as such, it can evoke a reaction and a response from anyone who sees it.

The distinction between reaction and response will come up again and again in the discussion of the effect and the usefulness of representational materials.

In very basic terms, *reaction* is the first, subjective, thing that happens on encountering the object (or text) in question. The expression of that reaction, in more or less considered terms, becomes the rather more objective *response*. And that response may, at its simplest, be 'l don't like it.' At its most complex level, the response may be critical exegesis; at the academic level, an essay or commentary. What interests us in the present context is closer to the simple level of expressing likes and dislikes, although, as will become clear, it should go quite a way beyond that.

In order to provoke a reaction and a response, the initial stimulus must attract the receiver's attention sufficiently to communicate something.

In non-verbal communication, some visual or aural impact must be made such that the receiver understands that something is being expressed. A response will be generated if this expression reaches the receiver at a level of involvement or interest. Then a kind of interaction can begin between receiver and text, viewer and image, reader and icon. In a non-educational context, the response is unconditioned, although the surrounding context, the company in which the receiver finds him—or herself, cultural awareness, expectations and background knowledge all come into play, and will influence to a greater or lesser extent the reactions and responses elicited. There is hardly ever a totally 'innocent' response to visual stimuli—we are expected to find Venice or the Taj Mahal breathtaking, pictures of famine victims shocking, and so on. But these cultural expectations in no way invalidate the contact with the material seen and responded to.

In the same way, in a classroom context, any visual material invites imaginative collaboration between student and image. This collaboration will be expressed in words, no matter what the original form of expression was. (It can also lead to further creative expression in visual or other forms, but that is beyond the scope of this book.)

The point of contact *at any level of linguistic capability* will be what has caught the imagination of the producer of the original image (photographer, artist, architect, or whatever). Not by chance are 'imagination' and 'image' closely linked, even etymologically. For it is that contact which reaches the receiver's imagination and stimulates *in the imagination* the reaction and response.

In language learning, the aim of using representational materials is to take advantage of that contact, to develop and exploit it, in words which will express feelings, emotions, judgements, and opinions, and which will reflect a degree of involvement with the images under discussion, and by extension, with the world they represent.

Representational materials contain some kind of vision of the object presented or described; they contain some point of contact between producer and receiver. That may simply be a question of selection: Why did the photographer decide to photograph this or that particular moment? But it may also reflect much deeper questions, involving ideas about the world, suggesting new levels of response and interaction.

Ideational materials are materials which try to encompass ideas which in normal circumstances would be difficult to express. What ideas does an enigmatic icon like Leonardo's *Mona Lisa* evoke or inspire, for instance? Reactions and responses can be basic or complex, just as the images to which one reacts and responds can be of infinite variety. Laughter is a reaction that is just as valid as discursive excogitation. There is a place for seriousness just as there is a place for light-heartedness.

What will always be of primary importance in the educational context is that the image be *didactically useful,* that the teacher and the learner alike can derive some benefit from working with this piece of visual 'text', that the words they are stimulated to use about the 'text' be a valid contribution to their overall language-learning objectives.

There is no shortage of books on the usefulness and exploitation of non-verbal materials in language learning. The intention of the present book, however, is to relate the *whole* process of working with representational materials to language learning. Non-verbal materials are only the tip of the iceberg, the starting-point for work with a vast range of verbal materials (reading texts) which, in the same way, open up possibilities for interaction, reaction and response, where what has caught the imagination of the producer of the message (the writer, in most cases) will be what stimulates the receiver, or reader, to talk, discuss, evaluate, accept, reject, and learn.

Imagination is the meeting-point. It is where input, verbal or non-verbal, stimulates interaction. And that is where involved learning begins, where language acquisition is most readily encouraged, where education draws out from the students an interest and an involvement in what they are working with—instead of imposing ideas and viewpoints on them.

Verbal materials

At an elementary level of language learning, great success has been achieved with young learners through the use of cartoon and puppet characters, most notably the Sesame Street characters. The success of such methods is due to *identification transfer;* that is, the young learner identifies the fictional character, and transfers the character's role from that of a character viewed for entertainment to that of a character along with whom a finding-out/learning process can be engaged in. Both learner and characters take on new roles vis-à-vis the characters' original function, although the entertainment value of the characters is fundamental to the learner's acceptance of the transfer of roles and identification.

This is an extreme example of how didactic objectives are rendered acceptable to the learner; the trick of identification transfer of this kind is as old as the educational process. Aesop's fables work on a not dissimilar principle—if the fable is applied to a real life context, a lesson or moral can be drawn from it.

In the present context, we are less interested in drawing a moral than in the way such identification transfer is relevant to the language-learning context. And the first step is to show how words need not remain on the merely referential level, but can take on new identities for a multiplicity of purposes—and, in their new guises, help us see familiar things in a new light. Words can play, just as Sesame Street characters can; and they can help us learn, if we allow them the freedom of expression and identity to 'represent' or stand for something, rather than simply referring to a fixed concept or object.

Language practice material with a touch of imagination

Much language practice material is mechanical and repetitive— even in up-to-date textbooks which make all the right communicative noises, are well illustrated, have good storylines, recurring characters, and so on. The boredom quotient in teaching materials is being diminished in the current glut of supplementary materials on the market, but there is no real reason why basic practice material cannot be methodologically sound *and* contain a touch of humour or the possibility of imaginative involvement.

This story, for example, is a never-ending one. It can be used at an elementary level, for simple reading, or with *wh-* questions as follow-up. A pre-reading question might ask students, as they read, to find how many characters there are.

Albert is a lorry driver. Every day he travels from his home in Birmingham to other parts of Great Britain.

Albert loves Eleanor; she is a young woman of twenty who works in a shoe shop and she lives in Wolverhampton, a town near Birmingham. Unfortunately, Eleanor doesn't love Albert.

Albert buys her flowers; he writes letters to her from

Glasgow, Cornwall, London, and Liverpool. He says, 'Eleanor, I love you. I don't want anyone else.' But she doesn't love him.

Eleanor loves Edward. Edward is a postman, and he delivers letters from Albert to Eleanor. Unfortunately, Edward doesn't love Eleanor.

Edward loves Helga, a Swedish waitress in a motorway restaurant. He drives to her restaurant in his car and asks her, 'Do you love me?' But she always says, 'No, I don't,' because Helga is in love with Albert.

Albert is a lorry driver. . .

Follow-up questions along the lines of, *Who loves/doesn't love whom?*, jobs etc., are obvious. What is not so immediately obvious is the long-term memory students will have on this 'eternal rectangle'!

The next story is simpler, and uses the past tense for practice and reinforcement. However, a pre-reading question like, *As you read, find out who the rebel is,* adds an element of spice to the simple tale.

Janet was nineteen years old in 1990. She was a very pretty girl and liked green fields, flowers, and fresh air.

Her father, Thomas, was very happy with his daughter and gave her money to buy good clothes and to have holidays in exotic places.

Janet had a boyfriend. His name was Robert, and he worked for her father as an accountant.

Then Janet met Jack. Jack liked to drink and smoke; he was a rebel, and Thomas hated him. Janet liked him. She started to see him more and more and was bored with Robert.

Janet started smoking, and she often went to bars with Jack. When her father gave her money, she gave it to Jack.

Robert didn't want to see her, and her father was very unhappy.

One day Jack and Janet went away on his motorbike and didn't return.

Procedural questions like: *Who was an accountant? Who worked for Thomas? Did Jack work for Thomas? Did Janet marry Robert? Who did Thomas like? Who gave money to Janet? Who did Janet give money to? How did Jack and Janet go away?* etc. can lead to prediction exercises: *What do you think happened next? What do you think happened to Robert?* and so on. In this way, the characters are brought to life and begin to exist in students' minds so that they can be referred to again, even some time after the past tense unit has been completed.

The story can be continued, using recall of the characters, to lead into an ongoing saga (or soap opera!).

On the night of November 17th 1990, Thomas, Janet's father, was sleeping alone in his house (his wife was dead) when he heard a noise and woke up.

He was an intelligent man, and he didn't run downstairs as soon as he heard the noise, but waited. He wanted to know how many people were in the house.

He got up very slowly and went to the bedroom door, opened it quietly, and put his head out. Then he stepped out into the hall and walked silently to the top of the stairs.

To his surprise, when he looked down, he saw his daughter, Janet, and her boyfriend, Jack. He watched them break into his safe, his drinks cupboard, and finally into his dining room where he had a lot of valuable antiques.

As soon as he saw them break into the dining room, he went back into his bedroom and telephoned the police.

They came quickly, and Jack and Janet were arrested. Janet began to cry and tried to talk to her father, but he didn't listen. When the police left, Thomas went back to bed and slept quietly.

Comprehension questions can lead to motivation questions: *Why did Jack and Janet come back? Why did Thomas phone the police?* Students are thus encouraged to get into the minds of the characters a little. A title could now be discussed, as well as further prediction exercises, perhaps leading to a happy ending (or not!), as students wish.

The next passage makes correcting errors fun, while practising tenses.

I walks down the street one day when I seen something strange. There was a man had a conversation with a dog.

The dog is big and black, probably an Alsatian, and it looked as if it understands everything the man is talking about.

'My wife don't understand me,' I had heard the man say. 'She is being bad to me for years, and I'm going to leave her. You understand me, don't you, Bengo?'

The dog wagged his tail in sympathy and looked at his boss.

'I'm going to leave her tomorrow,' he repeated. 'I take the taxi to the station, then a train to the airport. At the airport, I buy a ticket to Rio, and I arrive in time for the Carnival.'

'You've drunk too much,' said the dog.

'Why?' asks the man. 'How do you know?'

'Because everyone knows the Rio Carnival is last week,' replied Bengo. 'Come on, took me home!'

Students can be asked to retell the story in their own words, or to discuss its humour and absurdity. Bengo can become quite a character!

Finally, a story with a moral. What differences can you find between Barry and Harold?

Barry Masters and Harold Minton had very little in common. Barry came from the backstreets of Wolverhampton (an industrial town in the Midlands of England), while Harold was brought up in rural Kent, an affluent area south of London.

Barry's education was one of crime and violence. He spent most of his teens in Borstal for assorted crimes, ranging from snatching handbags to selling drugs.

Harold, on the other hand, attended private schools and, at the age of eighteen, entered Oxford University to study law.

Barry's later life continued in the same way. Prison was his most regular address, and he usually committed more offences soon after being released. As an ex-convict, it was almost impossible for him to find a job. Crime seemed to be the only solution, but the result was always the same.

Harold did well at university and made a good career for himself as a lawyer. He specialised in prosecution work.

The two men met in September 1983. Harold was the prosecuting lawyer, and Barry was charged with the armed robbery of a jeweller's shop. Barry was found guilty and sentenced to fifteen years imprisonment, the longest sentence of his life.

Before being led off to prison, Barry went to the toilet. He escaped through a window and went to look for Harold. He found him in an office of the court, and murdered him with his bare hands.

This lends itself splendidly to 'what if' exercises. *What would have happened if... Barry had been richer? ... Harold had been poorer?... Barry hadn't gone to Borstal? ...Harold had studied medicine? ...Barry*

hadn't been found guilty of armed robbery? ...Harold had gone home immedi-
ately after the trial? etc.

It is a small step from language-targeted materials like these to texts chosen for more specifically imaginative stimulation: songs, advertisements, visuals, and so on.

Comics and cartoons

For many teachers, comics and cartoons are the first imaginative materials they use, especially with younger and adolescent learners. There is no reason at all why this should not be so, but there are several important provisos.

First, there is the copyright question. In many countries, local publishers blatantly re-use Disney, Superman, Dandy, Beano, Asterix, Snoopy and the like in their original form. This is often illegal, as it is without (usually costly) copyright permission being obtained from the original copyright holders. The alternatives, which are imitations or near copies of identifiable originals, often do not have the appeal to students which familiar originals are bound to have.

With original cartoon materials, there can also be an accessibility problem, especially in terms of idiomatic use, cultural reference, and vocabulary. These problems can sometimes overwhelm the desired accessibility quotient, and lead to the student's rejection of the material.

Rejection can happen for a multitude of reasons, but most often, the reasons students give for rejecting an item will not actually be the deep reason. Students are naturally reluctant to admit, especially with visually accessible material, that it is 'difficult' or incomprehensible; so, dullness, boredom, or over-familiarity will often be adduced to cover up basic accessibility problems.

So, 'yes!' to Superman—but with modified rapture. Like any other imaginative materials, cartoon input has to be very carefully selected for the class/level it is to be used with. And, beware, it can date much more quickly than many other kinds of material. Transitoriness or ephemeral appeal can be a grave risk, a two-edged weapon. (ET and Adrian Mole were sadly transitory, for example, in holding adolescent student interest.) Trying too hard to meet young and adolescent learners' tastes is a high-risk area; equally risky is the imposition of teacher taste. The room for manoeuvre is limited, but not at all dangerously restrictive.

Songs

Songs can be very useful representational material. Most teachers are familiar with the requests from students to translate hit records or tracks from albums and videos. Many also use traditional or folk songs, children's songs, and nursery rhymes (for younger learners), and even specially written language-learning songs.

The reasons for using songs are well-known and hardly need to be gone into again here. Familiarity; accessibility; memorability; the close links between sound and sense, rhythm and rhyme, melody and meaning; and simple, enjoyable language practice are all valid reasons for using songs.

Less often, a song is used because its lyrics can be a useful stimulus. At that point, the song becomes a representational text and is as exploitable a material for interpretation and discussion as any other imaginative text. The best such songs usually contain a basic element of 'story', or a character clash, a point of view, an engagement with a social or other issue.

Many of the Beatles' songs have been in use in language classrooms for over twenty years. 'She's Leaving Home', 'Eleanor Rigby', and others have found their way into textbooks and have been exploited in numerous ways. Michael Jackson's 'Thriller' brought about a veritable explosion of language-learning related activities, covering drama, homemade video, story-telling, and creative writing. The mood of the moment often throws up highly stimulating material; and it will often be the students who will suggest to the teacher that use might be made of a song, album, or video.

The songs of Bob Dylan, Elvis Costello, and Billy Bragg, among others, offer wide-ranging possibilities for social or political engagement, although with some songs there is the risk that they may be too context-specific. However, subjects like freedom, political repression, minority views, and love relationships are of perennial interest, and a teacher will soon be able to judge a class's tastes and the kind of material they will respond well to.

A word of warning: we are all happy to use any song to fill in the last ten minutes of the last lesson of the week, but a distinction has to be made, in both the teacher's and the students' minds, between material used for its entertainment value (with maybe a bit of translation or explanation of the lyrics) and material which can be used more constructively for exploitation and interaction. Not that there is anything wrong with entertainment—quite the opposite! Entertainment is frequently sadly lacking in the classroom. But it is useless to pretend, to yourself or to your students, that the latest disco hit is any more than just that.

Naturally, for exploitation purposes, lyric sheets are necessary, or a projection of them. After hearing the song without reading the lyrics, the words can be read in silence, the song heard again, and the usual procedure for representational materials followed. It is usually demotivating to read the lyrics before or during the first hearing of the song (differently, therefore, from ordinary written texts): the first hearing arouses the listeners' curiosity, such that they are motived to read. A few words or phrases may have been picked out at first hearing (perhaps the pre-hearing stimulus could suggest that this is what they do), and these can be discussed before the reading proceeds.

If social issues and the like are raised, the song becomes the textual reference point for all the continuing work. The music itself should not, of course, be ignored, as it is an integral part of the song as text, as opposed to the lyrics as text. How well the music reflects or relates to the lyric, how the arrangement, tone of voice, and production help the lyrics—such questions can enrich the discussion.

One hidden advantage of the use of songs lies in their use of variant, often dialect, forms. Varieties of English—from soul to rap, from schmaltz to scouse—can be found in songs. These need not be taught as such or even analysed in any depth. What is important is student exposure to these wide-ranging varieties; to the way 'rules' are broken; to differences between written and spoken (or, here, sung) forms; to colloquial, local, sectorial, racial, social, and regional expression in English.

This bears out Halliday's highly significant distinction between speaking and writing which, he says, give 'two complementary perspectives; the *synoptic* and the *dynamic*' (Halliday, 1985/1989: 97). The written language presents a synoptic view of the world, defining it as 'product rather than process'. The spoken language presents a dynamic view, defining 'its universe primarily as process'. It is the language of phenomena as they happen. Songs, especially pop songs, have this dynamic quality, which it can often be useful to relate to other more static, more synoptic texts, written to be read on a page rather than heard with music.

The best use of songs as representational material will always involve comparison and contrast with other texts, rather than simply handling the individual song in isolation. The song can be part of a theme-based set of texts or can be related to visual stimuli, to advertisements, or to other songs. Continuity of exposure to representational materials implies this range of text types, and songs are among the very best motivational texts we can find.

It is perhaps even more important with songs than with other kinds of imaginative texts for the teacher not to impose or inflict his or her own tastes on the students. Folk songs are usually popular, and there are some packages of out-of-copyright songs on the market. Pop music is fraught with ephemera—and there is a generation gap danger here, quite apart from likes and dislikes!

Without wishing to fall into the trap of inflicting personal tastes on others, I offer a list of some of the songs which I have found most constantly and recurringly useful over the years (ephemeral successes are left out!).

- 'Father and Son' (Cat Stevens)
- 'In the Ghetto' (Elvis Presley)
- 'The Ballad of the Absent Mare' (Leonard Cohen)
- 'I am ... I Said' (Neil Diamond)
- 'Eve of Destruction' (Barry McGuire)
- 'Blowin' in the Wind' (Bob Dylan)
- 'New York' (Lou Reed)
- 'Love Letters in the Sand' (Pat Boone, and others)
- 'Glad to Be Gay' (Tom Robinson Band)
- 'What's Love Got to Do With It?' (Tina Turner)

All of these can be easily and clearly related to themes, discussion topics, or social issues, without either forcing the song to be what it is not or cheapening the issue involved. Obviously, the choice reflects a part of just one teacher's taste and experience— every teacher could add another Top Ten to this one.

Advertisements

Advertisements are just as much texts as any other kind of material. They have an 'authorial' producer of the message just as literary texts do; but they have a much less open textual purpose than the open texts of imaginative writing. They are useful in the way they use word-play, point of view, the receiver's affective

suggestibility, and they help students to learn to read and understand the propaganda of persuasion.

Approaches to advertisement should consider both image(s)
and the text, and should examine:

- What the advertisement is trying to do;
- Who (and what) it is appealing to;
- Its overt and subliminal appeal;
- Its success and otherwise (does it work on the students?
  Why, or why not?);
- Are its plays on words clear to L2 speakers, or are they
  obscure?
- How does the advertisement compare with
  advertisements in the students' own language(s)?

What is being looked at, interacted with, discussed, and evaluated here is a very clear category of representational materials,
which are designed to convince and persuade. Therefore the *intention* is usually clear from the outset, which is not normally the case
with fictional materials. What is studied, then, is *how* the text
works, rather than *what* it is about or what issues it raises.

The usefulness of advertisements is, by this token, limited; but
they are not to be despised. Their appeal is a direct one, often an
emotional one, and the range of subtle and less subtle means of
persuasion—and the feelings these means play upon—make
reading advertisements a necessary talent to develop in a mass-
media dominated world.

'One-liners'

Very brief quotations, or 'one-liners', can be very useful in stimulating class interest in a subject (introducing a theme or even an
author, for instance) or in provoking class discussion (agree-

ing/disagreeing, interpreting and evaluating, and so on). Consider these:

- Experience is the name everyone gives to their mistakes.
- I wonder men dare trust themselves with men.
- Monday's child is fair of face, Tuesday's child is full of grace.
- Oh, East is East, and West is West, and never the twain shall meet.
- Words are, of course, the most powerful drug used by mankind.
- 'Tis said that some have died for love.
- Comparisons are odorous.
- Candy is dandy, but liquor is quicker.
- Continental people have sex life; the English have hot-water bottles.
- One religion is as true as another.
- How can the bird that is born for joy / Sit in a cage and sing?
- Strange how potent cheap music is.

These are quite different from the short extracts in the previous chapter. These quotations assert and affirm: a truth, an opinion, a popular belief, or a witty apothegm. They can be exploited in a number of ways.

- What do they mean, and what do they refer to? (*comprehension/interpretation*)
- Do students agree or disagree? Why, or why not? (*discussion*)
- How else could the concept be expressed? (*reformulation*)
- Used as stimulus for writing or debate. (*extension*)

- Used for language description. ('Tis *as archaic/poetic, for example*)
- Classified as humorous, sententious, true, irrelevant, old-fashioned, etc. *(evaluation)*
- Given separately to pairs or groups for them to explain to the rest of the class, either as a memory game after first acquaintance (*Can you remember three words, speaking about comparing?* for example) or presenting the general idea first, leading to the concise quotation ('One religion is as true as another.'). *(language exploitation)*
- To show how strong affirmation depends on simple verbs (largely the present tense of *to be* and *to have*), or on rhetoric (as in the final example). *(language)*

These affirmations can be contrasted with deliberately controversial one-liners, such as:

- I can resist everything except temptation.
- No civilized man ever regrets a pleasure, and no uncivilized man ever knows what a pleasure is.
- We are all in the gutter, but some of us are looking at the stars.
- Art never expresses anything but itself.
- Each man kills the thing he loves.
- One should never trust a woman who tells one her real age.
- In matters of grave importance, style, not sincerity, is the vital thing.
- A man cannot be too careful in his choice of enemies.
- It is only shallow people who do not judge by appearances.
- There is no sin except stupidity.
- Chastity is the most unnatural of all the sexual

perversions.

- Gentlemen prefer blondes.
- I could love anything on earth that appeared to wish it.
- Power tends to corrupt, and absolute power corrupts absolutely. Great men are almost always bad men.
- Man is the only creature that consumes without producing.
- War is Peace; Freedom is Slavery; Ignorance is Strength.
- If all the year were playing holidays, to sport would be as tedious as to work.
- The cruellest lies are often told in silence.
- It is impossible, in our condition of society, not to be sometimes a snob.

The fact that the first ten of these are by the same writer— Oscar Wilde—might encourage students towards reading more of his works; although that is not, obviously, the main object of using one-liners. They are deliberately paradoxical, teasing, sometimes contradictory. The range of exploitation possibilities in class is slightly greater than with the purely affirmative one-liners we saw earlier; they might go on to encompass:

- for and against (*discussion*)
- true or false? (*evaluation*)
- Who is trying to convince whom? (*point of view*)
- Where is the contradiction, and why is it valid? (*interpretation/relevance*)
- Is it humorous, true, both, or neither? (*opinion*)

Students find themselves almost immediately having to justify their opinions, reactions, and responses. They have to go beyond the initial, largely subjective reaction and try to formulate some kind of more considered response, not only to the text itself but to their colleagues' reactions and responses to it. Interaction spreads from reader/text to reader/text/other reader(s), and possibly also (writer)/reader/text/other reader(s)/teacher. The process is an ongoing one, with no definite end necessarily prescribed.

Proverbs

Some teachers enjoy using proverbs in this way, since they can often be related to similar sayings in students' own languages and discussed, therefore, with some degree of the familiarity of known territory. Clearly, overly idiomatic expressions should be avoided, but some useful examples are:

- It is an ill wind turns none to good. (Perhaps better known as 'It's an ill wind that blows nobody any good.')
- A bird in the hand is worth two in the bush.
- Those whom the Gods love die young.
- It's love that makes the world go round.
- If it isn't true, it ought to be.
- If there was no God, we'd have to invent him.
- (Not only) fine feathers make fine birds.
- (He is) a wolf in sheep's clothing.
- He who laughs last laughs longest.
- He who laughs last is the last to see the joke.

These sayings offer variants, misreadings, and twists which allow for a range of reaction and response, especially in the context of L1/L2 contrast. Students will probably offer further examples, which may or may not have equivalents in English. There is, however, the risk of sententiousness with this kind of folk wisdom. Its interest value is limited, and students should be encouraged to go to more 'controversial' material before the attraction of proverbs begins to pall.

Idioms

Idioms present an area of language use that is analogous to this, but they carry with them a range of risks which preclude their being taught in any systematic way. An expression such as *He blew his top* is, in fact, a metonymic use of representational language, with a mechanical explosion of some kind as its referent. An L2 student will find considerable difficulty in *not* immediately relating *He blew his top* to the more familiar, referential *He blew his nose*. Carry this on to idioms like *blowing his own trumpet* and an area of L2 difficulty becomes apparent. The difficulty is cultural rather than lexical.

Too much idiomatic language in a representational text can make the text impenetrable. Register, dialect, and background reference are the main areas where this problem can arise—but how to cope with it is a question that has long troubled materials writers and teachers. A wealth of dictionaries of idioms gives students lexicographical points of reference—and their use is to be encouraged, in smallish doses.

The point is, however, that there is no real need for students to be able to *use* idioms actively. Idioms can easily become part of students' passive knowledge, as reading familiarity grows. But frequency of use in spoken or written English depends on how appropriate or apposite the idiom is in a given situation; and the ability to judge such suitability in active production implies a very advanced sensitivity to language use, culture, and register, which is not within most learners' scope.

Clearly, some familiarity with idioms and how they work will develop as a natural part of language learning, and regular use of representational materials will aid this considerably. But the artificiality of the kind of L2 production that is exemplified by *It's not my cup of tea, but I'm putting my best foot forward and my nose to the grindstone, though my back is to the wall* is to be avoided at all costs!

Idioms can be explained or checked with a dictionary as they occur, and as and when necessary. Practice in the use of them is, I feel, a false learning technique. They will be reinforced only by familiarity with usage, rather than by repetition in artificial, largely referential contexts.

Readers

Despite Tricia Hedge's well-argued and spirited championing of graded readers that present reduced versions of original texts, I have to register several objections. It is in the nature of such readers that the original text has been rendered more 'accessible' by the elimination or facilitation of the kind of difficulty factors we have discussed. Yet there is something inherently contradictory in wishing to present the 'whole' text in a filleted form. This is not to deny access to George Eliot's *Silas Marner* to all who wish to read it: such a text is not the province of only the more advanced student, as should be clear by now. My point is that a graded reader, despite the advantage of containing all of the story, is a pale replica, a watered-down version, of the original. It is the *what* but not the *how*, the tale but not the telling.

Working with George Orwell's *Nineteen Eighty-Four*, for example, I have found the following experience salutary. On page two of the novel, as part of Orwell's description of London, we come across the word *grimy*. This is a word L2 readers may very well not have come across previously (one of many in the opening pages of the novel). If students consult a dictionary—especially one of the pocket bilingual dictionaries they often encumber themselves with —they will like as not find a suggested familiar synonym, *dirty*, or the usual word for *dirty* in their own language. But Orwell deliberately did not use *dirty*; he used *grimy*. It is perhaps simplistic, but none the less valid, to assert that, in terms of lexical choice and desired effect, literature *is* the difference between *dirty* and *grimy*.

The very unfamiliarity and, frequently, the unexpectedness of the author's choice of words or of structures is what makes an imaginative text different from a purely referential piece of language use.

Authorial choice depends on many factors, not the least of which is point of view. There is a clear relation between how the writer sees what he is writing about and how he or she wants the reader to see the same thing. The choices an author makes—what to write about and *how* to write about it—are fundamental to the text the reader receives. And what we might call 'desired effect'— in the most open sense possible, the impact the text has on its reader—depends very much on these authorial choices. The effect may hardly ever be exactly the one consciously or unconsciously desired by the author, as it will involve such mysterious intangibles as the reader's receptive context—social, educational, linguistic, cultural, etc. The reader, interpreting or (as Barthes would have it) 'rewriting' the text, is necessarily filtering the authorial choices through all the receptive mechanisms and conditions in the context of which he or she is confronted with the text. Reading alone or in class, on a train or in bed, for study purposes or for pleasure, alert or dozy, comfortable or uncomfortable, politically secure or afraid, emotionally stable or susceptible, linguistically confident or not—all these (and more) are contributory factors to how the text will affect the reader.

Graded readers which are purpose-written *up* to the level of the student, rather than brought *down* to students' language-learning needs, are of course an immensely valuable source of representational material, both for class use and for extensive reading. With low-level graded readers, students can be introduced to complete texts for reading at a very early stage.

In most teaching situations, only short texts can be read intensively in class; but the use of graded readers (and all extensive reading) can and should be monitored in class time, as well as actively encouraged outside class time.

Extensive reading

Extensive reading implies that students read outside the classroom fuller texts than the passages examined in class for purely language-learning purposes. The materials can be anything from graded readers to short stories to full-length works of fiction or non-fiction.

This implies reading for pleasure, even though the reading programme may be formulated or guided by the teacher. Text selection by the teacher in such cases will be important, as will specific enabling lessons or exercises to help the reading (as, for example, the Edinburgh Extensive Reading Project and the Penguin Extensive Reading Programme are working to provide).

Language learning, as such, is a spin-off from extensive reading, rather than the other way round. Reading makes a considerable contribution to language learning, but in a global rather than in a specific way. Discrete items of language (vocabulary, syntax, or whatever) will only rarely actually be *learned* during extensive reading, unless they are noted down in a student's reading diary or handled in a workbook or class exercise. But *language acquisition* is being reinforced throughout the extensive reading, whether it be of one text per year or twenty; and *language awareness* is being helped while reading outside the class—especially if the student is following a course which exploits representational materials.

Extensive reading is, first and foremost, a matter of enthusiasm; and generally that enthusiasm must be transmitted from the teacher to the students. The students' own reading will become part of their self-development as well as of their language learning, and the process of extensive reading—in L1 or L2—may continue as part of students' continuing education.

6 TEXT SELECTION

To be usable and valid, a short text must have a clear and readily identifiable setting, and/or situation, and/or characters. Any one of these can be sufficient. What happens, or what is said, must involve some element of narrative or dramatic tension. In some sense, there will almost always be a turning point in the passage, something that will indicate a movement within the passage, implying a beginning, a middle, and an end.

A purely descriptive passage will be the exception to this rather vague but general rule. In fact, the usefulness of purely descriptive writing is limited in an L2 context for this very reason—that is, the lack of clearly defined movement within the text.

The selection of imaginative texts for use in language teaching is difficult, controversial, and ultimately pretty subjective. The criteria for text selection are manifold, and probably every individual teacher would place the important points that follow in a different order of importance.

Any text choice may be challenged on many counts—and indeed this includes the mere fact of the teacher choosing texts for the students' consumption—but such role-instigated direction of students' reading is inherent in the teaching process. If we bear in mind that the ideal goal is learner autonomy in the target language, the teacher's success in working towards this goal becomes the touchstone.

Accessibility

Hardly any imaginative text is instantly accessible to the foreign language reader. Indeed, many imaginative texts are less than immediately accessible to native tongue readers. The use of authentic newspaper materials in language teaching has shown the considerable problems of register, inference, and allusion, which render inaccessible to L2 readers such seemingly simple uses of English as headlines and reportage—and the most popular papers create the greatest difficulties.

This reflects how the use of idiom, word-play, and cultural contextualisation in everyday language calls upon a much wider frame of reference than students are normally faced with. The decoding of newspaper English, while frequently a stimulating exercise in finding out, has an interest level that is closely dependent upon the interest of the story contained within the popular register. And if, as can easily happen, there is not very much to the story, the battle to make it accessible to the L2 learner often seems more trouble than it is worth. We return to the perennial question: What has the student actually learned?

Accessibility depends more on how the reading text is presented than on any of the multiplicity of linguistic and cultural factors which may render it inaccessible. Students will often react negatively to a text because they have been understandably daunted by its register, its syntax, unknown vocabulary, the culture gap—any of a dozen stumbling blocks which make it infinitely easier for a learner to give up on a text than to make it through to the end.

Accessibility, therefore, depends very much on making the student capable of getting through the text to the end. This is one of the main reasons I strongly advocate the use of recordings of all kinds of representational texts. The advantages may seem obvious, but are worth considering at length.

First, listening while reading the text dispels the feeling that this kind of reading is somehow a variant on reading comprehension: it is clearly neither listening comprehension nor reading comprehension, simply the presentation of a text.

Secondly, listening while reading means students have to follow the text through to the end or to a stopping-point determined by the teacher. This avoids the kind of hold-ups caused by finger-reading, by puzzling over unknown words, and by similar kinds of disorientation.

It also has the inestimable virtue of demonstrating to the students themselves that they can get through a text which, in other circumstances, might have seemed inaccessible. To give a quick example: most native speakers will find themselves (albeit momentarily) in difficulty with this sentence if presented with it baldly thus:

It was and I said not but.

Non-native speakers will more than likely be baffled by it, until they hear it spoken or see it properly punctuated:

'It was "and",' I said, 'not "but".'

The following line presents a standard problem of comprehension in L2 students' frequent miscollocation of the final gerund— often it will be read as if it were an adjective:

One man was just folded over a tree weeping.

Intonation and stress will avoid any temptation to interpret the tree as a willow, and will render the gerund as the verb it should be.

Very often the non-native reader depends upon the reading aloud of the text to overcome such potential perplexities which, for the most part, have become part of a native speaker's reading techniques; the placing of a verb, the collocation of an adjective, the stress and rhythm of a line, all can present problems to the L2 reader. Certainly these can be puzzled out, but it is precisely the feeling of puzzlement that we want to eliminate. The exercise should *not* be a technical one of deciphering. Listening to a recording helps greatly in the L2 reader's process of cognition—in finding out, rather than working out, some of the basic ways in which the text works and some of the basic things it is doing.

Of course, the objection can be raised that any reading or recording presents an interpretation of the text, and thereby influences the listener/ reader's reception and understanding of it. This is inevitable, and in no way unacceptable. The advantages considerably outweigh the drawbacks, however. Interpretation is fundamental to this kind of material: as the novelist George Eliot put it, 'All meanings, we know, depend on the key of interpretation.'

Reading representational materials is reading as a function of the imagination, so interpretation is to be encouraged rather than avoided. Discussion of how a recording presents an interpretation, acceptable or otherwise, can become a regular part of the exercise.

Accessibility is increased by careful instruction as to what the student should do with the text. The student gains a great deal of confidence if he or she can (a) get through to the end of the text, then (b) do the task, or answer the question, set on it. So the reader must be clear from outset what he or she has to do with this text: find the names of the characters, decide where it is set, work out relationships, etc. Basic *wh-* questions (*who, where, what,* and possibly—but usually more problematically—*why*) give the simplest and most basic of such stimuli.

Clearly the context in which any text is presented will also have a lot to do with its accessibility to students. A text must be seen as part of a course, or relevant to a subject under discussion, rather than just produced out of the blue without any clear point of reference.

Difficulty

This is perhaps the most controversial aspect of all discussions of representational language, especially if there is anything remotely 'literary' in the texts under discussion.

There is a kind of received wisdom that 'literature' is the province of upper-intermediate and advanced language students, *if any at all*. A kind of barrier is raised somewhere around 'good intermediate' level, close to the University of Cambridge Local Examinations Syndicate's First Certificate level, after which students are felt to be more able to cope with 'literary' texts. This is a false division, one that is reinforced rather than diminished by the Syndicate's literary options, which seem to run more or less directly counter to Jonathan Culler's famous assertion, 'our examinations are not designed merely to check whether [the student] has read and remembered certain books but to test his or her progress as a reader of literature.' (In Schiff (ed.) 1977:64.)

However, it is not my intention here to take issue with any institution's examining system—though testing, or verification, is a subject we must return to later in the book. Rather, the point at issue is how early in L2 learning ideational and representational materials can be brought into a course. Some of my arguments have already been given under the heading of 'Accessibility'.

What happens when L2 students look at a new text? If it is in the context of their learning situation, students will assume that the text is at least relevant to their language-learning competence, and that they should normally be able to get something beneficial out of their reading. That 'something' has been established by the teacher or textbook writer who prepared the materials. If the text is designed as reading comprehension, it should be carefully attuned to the level of the course the student has reached, probably stretching the learner a little in terms of vocabulary, but giving him or her the possibility of answering the questions which follow the passage. Imaginative texts—purpose-written, simplified, or authentic—can be, and frequently are, used for reading comprehension, although, especially in ESP, the texts are likely to be more useful in the development of reading skills if they contain some element of focus on the student's specialisation.

The reading skills being developed through the use of texts for reading comprehension are rather different from those encouraged by ideational reading. Technical ability—to read for gist, to skim, to scan, to guess unknown words, to search for answers, to relate information and transform it as the question requires—is necessary in any reading context. The usefulness of reading comprehension as such necessarily diminishes as the individual student's technical competence mounts. There is inevitably the danger that the exercise can lose some of its value: students get into a reading comprehension habit (teachers do too!). Thus, a reading comprehension exercise can become a fill-in when there is some class time to spare: students and teacher are satisfied that something constructive has been done, a couple of pages covered, a group of questions answered. But if we ask again what the students have learned, the answer might be 'very little'. Reasoning, intuitive, and deductive processes are not generally made to work very hard in reading comprehension—the *thinking* skill is left undeveloped.

What the students bring to the text will contribute a great deal to this process: world knowledge, cultural background, personal experience, all play a part. It is the teacher's job, as Derek Brewer puts it (1984:13), 'to unite experience from within with instruction from without.' Instruction clearly goes beyond the mere technicalities of comprehension. To quote Brewer again (1984:8), 'We have to begin with the personal and merge it into the public domain, and ultimately re-integrate the public interest with the personal.'

Reading, beyond the necessary technical abilities required of the reader, has to involve some stimulus of cognitive and responsive processes. It is here that level becomes important. For the level of text that can be used depends very largely on what the students are asked to do with the text, rather than on any inherent grading problems. A text which would clearly be of Proficiency level if used as reading comprehension can be used at much lower levels if the apparatus and the demands made on the student are apposite to that lower level. Grading the *tasks* rather than the *texts* is vital.

Traditional ideas of reading competence lead to advanced students—post-Proficiency students even—merely displaying technical ability in comprehension, in question-answering, and in summarising. Any degree of involvement or interaction with the text is avoided. This is objectivity to a fault: subjectivity is necessary to interactive reading. An overemphasis on objectivity will develop only technical ability, and will result in problems of accessibility as soon as otherwise technically adept students are faced with even fairly simple texts that are open in interpretative possibilities.

Closed texts are fine for developing technical skills; open texts are necessary for the development of reading with interactive understanding and response, whatever the students' language level.

Story

The best texts contain some element of story. With the very shortest of texts, there is little scope for story-telling—although the building up, through students' suggestions, of a background, a situation, or character involvement can make a story of even a one-liner.

Stories are a fundamental part of human experience. As George Steiner put it, 'no tribe on earth is so wretched that it does not express its dreams, its hopes, its ambitions, its fears in stories.' And stories can be of any length. The following is an interesting one to examine.

> Two Dogs who had been fighting for a bone, without advantage to either, referred their dispute to a Sheep.
>
> The Sheep patiently heard their statements, then flung the bone into a pond.
>
> 'Why did you do that?' said the Dogs.
>
> 'Because,' replied the Sheep, 'I am a vegetarian.'

This story can be retold in many more accessible ways, eliminating the rather old-fashioned style. Many teachers would prefer to use it in this form:

> Two dogs were fighting over a bone. Neither of them could beat the other. So they told a sheep their problem.
>
> The sheep listened to them, and then threw the bone into a pond.
>
> 'Why did you do that?' said the dogs.
>
> 'Because,' replied the sheep, 'I am a vegetarian.'

The differences between the two stories are minimal: sentence length, the removal of dependent clauses and clefting, fewer capital letters, easier verbs. But the second version is decidedly easier, or more accessible, to L2 readers. If the verbs were in the present tense, it would be even more accessible to more readers.

However, I believe that once students have read whatever 'simplified' version the teacher decides to use, it is useful to have them compare it with the original. This is, of course, not possible with reduced versions of extended texts. But the principle still holds good that the comparison of some passages, between simplified and original versions, helps students into an understanding of how language can be richer/poorer, more complex/simpler, more or less modern, and so on.

The uninterrupted use of simplified materials can offer the stimulus of a story and can vitally encourage the development of reading skills and competence; but it offers no opportunity for this kind of language awareness development.

The greatest value of the use of stories in language teaching is in their encouragement of students towards extensive reading, towards reading for pleasure. *What will happen next?* is the basic motivation which keeps the reader interested—and keeps the reader reading.

The theme-based approach: for and against

As we have seen, careful text selection is fundamental to the successful use of any kind of representational materials. How these texts are then linked together is just as important.

Clearly, learning objectives will often dictate how texts are grouped. In a specifically literature-based programme, for example, the works of a period, a single writer, a group of writers, or of a genre might have to be studied. The Eighteenth Century, Shakespeare, the Metaphysical Poets, the Romantics, the Rise of the Novel are cases where limited curriculum requirements necessitate careful specialist selection of a suitably representative number of texts to be studied during a course.

For the non-literature specialist, the field is wide open, perhaps indeed too wide for some teachers. Many teachers of English feel restricted by their own limited reading and are wary of using texts by unfamiliar authors or from genres (poetry especially) with which they have had little to do. However, collections of short stories are one simple way of grouping texts by genre, and such collections are widely used; many of them, indeed, are united by theme (sea stories, childhood stories, war stories, love stories, and so on).

What has been called the theme-based approach helps considerably to overcome the doubts and fears in the teacher's mind. It permits the grouping together of the most diverse texts, of any period or genre, because of some (even fairly tenuous) thematic link between them.

There are many possible objections to such an approach, and they must be carefully examined. First, it can be objected that the approach is reductive. As Steven Connor says (1985:7), 'the term *theme* in common literary-critical usage denotes that general idea or preoccupation, be it ethical, philosophical, political or psychological, which the particulars of a text seem to reflect.' Of course, as Connor rightly warns, 'there are dangers of great crudeness in this approach.'

Choosing a passage from a novel, play or poem is already in a way diminishing the work as a whole. Choosing the passage for a theme may very well misrepresent the work from which it was taken, in that the theme under discussion may not have been any major concern of the author's in writing the text. Isolated texts do not necessarily represent their period or the traditions in which they were created. And the drawing out of similar themes from very different texts might run the risk of making the texts seem to resemble each other too much, or, conversely, make a text seem less successful in examining the theme and therefore less well-written than might otherwise be thought. Also, the very artificiality of putting diverse texts together can be challenged.

Each of these objections (and many others of a similar kind) has considerable validity. Literary specialists, in particular, often feel the theme-based approach trivialises the work from which it extrapolates a passage. Semioticians and deconstructionists have objected that close analysis of single texts is forfeited by the emphasis on the comparing and contrasting of texts and their thematic content. I have also been told, on more than one occasion, that the number of themes available is limited and the approach is therefore of limited usefulness; or that placing Wordsworth's 'Daffodils' beside texts by Roger McGough and Samuel Beckett is no way to approach either Romanticism, modern poetry, or modern drama.

All of these queries must be recognised and accepted as possible drawbacks inherent in the theme-based approach. But almost all of them can be countered, and the approach can be more than justified in practical and pragmatic terms as the most suitable way of using representational materials in an L2 context, as well as furnishing an introduction to the study of, or specialisation in, English literature for non-native speakers.

First of all, the thematic approach is enormously flexible: almost any text can be accommodated, and the juxtaposition of texts can lead to surprisingly interesting discoveries. For example, placing a passage from George Orwell's 1945 'fairy tale', *Animal Farm,* beside a passage narrating the fall of the rebel angels in john Milton's 1667 epic poem, *Paradise Lost,* brings out remarkable similarities in political context, the nature of rebellions, and the verbal techniques used by the authors to express violence. Equally valuable and stimulating are the contrasts which emerge from the juxtaposition of these two texts: contrasts in form, in style, in language, in tone, to name only the most obvious. The texts complement each other in this case. Of course, this will not happen in every case, but it can lead to very interesting and productive discoveries when it does.

The most important feature of using a theme-based approach must be that the theme emerges from the text, rather than the teacher or materials writer deliberately seeking out a text *about* a theme. What is Wordsworth's 'Daffodils' *about*, after all? Its inclusion in a group of texts could be justified for any number of themes: flowers, nature, the life of the mind, spring, the country contrasted with the city, solitude and/or loneliness, imagery, memory. None of these would distort the text in any way. Neither should the theme into which the text is worked impose itself so thoroughly on the text as to deny the reader the possibility of finding some of the other thematic openings contained in it.

Of course, a self-contained text, as we have already said, is easier to use than a passage extrapolated from its surrounding context. But the principle of thematic openness holds nonetheless. The text should not be constricted by its thematic labelling. Sometimes a passage may be found which is interesting from a stylistic or linguistic point of view but, because of its thematic openness, is very difficult to group with other texts. This can lead to grouping for stylistic or linguistic reasons.

A group of passages which display, let us say, lexical, syntactical or stylistic affinities, is no less usable than a group of texts united by theme. However, purely linguistic or stylistic grouping can limit the thematic potential of the text. Foregrounding of any feature of a text is possible with any kind of grouping. Thematic grouping has the advantage that it can leave room for the foregrounding of stylistic or syntactic features, where the contrary might not necessarily be true.

But what is a 'theme'? 'Description' is just as much a theme as 'love'; 'propaganda' is as usable a heading as 'family'. The heading given to a group of texts is only a guideline. What is done with the texts themselves is much more important.

That said, I have often found it necessary to reject attractive and interesting texts because I have been unable to find other suitable material to use them with. Very often, comparison or juxtaposition with another text brings out more from the text than at first seemed possible. The fundamental importance of point of view— whether narratorial, authorial, of character, or of reader—is what most significantly enters into play here. And it is this range of points of view that allows texts to be exploited, compared and contrasted, instead of merely being used as examples (or samples) of stylistic, lexical, or syntactical usage. The variants inherent in the style, syntax and lexis of any selection of texts become, therefore, a *part* of what the texts are used for, rather than being the *whole reason* for using them.

These elements can be seen as vitally contributing to the ways in which the meaning of the text is achieved and communicated: the *how* of the text, which obviously will relate closely to the *why* of the text. Theme-grouping indicates a possible *why* for the text but, as we have seen, not by any means the only one. Indeed, the best kind of thematic grouping is loose rather than binding. It gives the reader the opportunity to explore a selection of texts which are grouped together for a reason, but does not prejudice the autonomy of the individual texts. It gives a reason for reading, simply by virtue of the linking of the disparate texts. It is, in a sense, a suggestion of how the texts can be interpreted (i.e. by imposing the theme they might have in common), but the apparatus must question this very grouping if it is honestly to allow the full interpretative freedom that texts and readers deserve. It is a temporary means to a clearly defined end: to bring readers to as wide a range of textual experience as possible, while encouraging interaction, interpretation and the evaluation of the texts and their contents.

Frequently, and very satisfyingly for the teacher, students are stimulated to seek out the full text, of which they have read a passage, or other works by a writer they have encountered in the context of theme-based reading. The move towards extended reading should, in many teaching situations, be part of the objectives of a theme-based course.

The theme-based approach implies comparison; implies, therefore, evaluation. That is to say that the students, consciously or subconsciously, are rating texts as better/more interesting/less attractive than others. They are building up a subjective ability to distinguish between texts and the way they work on the reader. This process moves from a subconscious to an explicit comparative evaluation of what has been read.

The theme-based approach thus furnishes an introduction to the vast range of representational reading matter available to readers of English. A great many students will never go beyond this stage; so this exposure to and familiarisation with a spectrum of writing, by authors known and unknown, also implies a fair degree of teacher responsibility. Teachers often feel the urge to include some of the 'great names' of literature, so that students will at least know, for example, one little bit of Shakespeare. This is to put the cart before the horse: we must find the right texts first. Naturally, there are many splendidly exploitable texts by 'big-name' writers, but it is equally true that a lot of 'great writing' is just not usable with lower level L2 readers. A good random collection of usable passages will reflect: the selector's range of reading and preferences; a mix of known and unknown texts and authors; a sense of the unexpected (a small section from Pope's 'The Rape of the Lock' placed beside William Carlos William's 'Death the Barber', for instance); and a revelation that—as some theorists not altogether frivolously maintain—all texts seem to relate to one another, contributing to one great text which is no more and no less than the sum of our reading experience.

Text grouping

Text grouping is a fairly open field. Texts can be grouped together constructively under many kinds of heading which do not concern their thematic content: Argument, Narration, Humour, Reflection, Philosophy, are among many general headings available. There is, I feel, a danger of dispersiveness if a heading is too open. Linguistic groupings, focusing on specific language features, are also possible: speech acts, sound and sense, dialect, register, even punctuation, can be foregrounded in such groupings. Here the connections to be exploited between the texts will be linguistic and stylistic rather than content-based.

Of course, no extrapolated passage is autotelic, and the fact of text grouping leaves open the way in which the text will be exploited. To a certain extent, the grouping, titling, heading, or theme is just a convenience for the teacher or materials writer. That said, it is vital that grouping decisions be clearly communicated to the students. They must know why a particular text is being studied, and what relationship it has with other texts which have been or are to be studied.

In terms of language use, though, it is enormously difficult to group together texts which will usefully foreground, for example, noun phrases, verb phrases, the clause, or cohesion, while still retaining reading attractiveness, interest value, and comparative discussion and evaluation potential. A distinction has to be recognised between text selection for the purposes of *exemplification* (of linguistic features, etc.) and text selection for the purposes of language learning and interaction. Any text will contain single examples of separate features of linguistic and didactic interest, and the apparatus can exploit these (or not, as the case may be). But to find four or five texts wherein noun phrases are to be examined as the principal study element is both forced and demotivating.

Period grouping—eighteenth-century prose passages grouped together, for example—is much more likely to be didactically useful, both from the literary and from the linguistic point of view. However, as soon as a period focus is given, we are moving towards literary specialisation. The inclusion of passages from very different periods in a theme-linked grouping can lead to valuable comparative discussion and language awareness: indeed, I tend to feel that the use *only* of passages of contemporary English is rather limiting. Language does not exist in a historical vacuum, but specific historically based study of language and texts remains a specialised area of interest. Genre grouping is only likely to be useful in the more limited context of literature as specialised study.

The pleasure of the text

Reading literature in a second language is not an easy exercise, nor is it immediately a pleasure. The pleasure of extended reading in L2 is an ideal, an objective that both students and teachers would doubtless like to reach, but that, realistically, requires a lot of effort. Reading for pleasure in L1 is a question of decisions and choices: the reader decides fairly quickly whether or not to continue reading a particular book or writer. In L2, the reader is more inhibited about admitting defeat. 'Difficulty' might seem to be the problem; getting to the end of a novel, especially a pre-twentieth-century triple-decker, is a daunting prospect! (Not that it isn't for L1 readers too!)

There is the basic problem of intrinsic interest. There is probably no subject that will interest a sample of students from San Diego, Southampton, Aarhus, Ankara, Addis Ababa, Asuncion, Bradford, and Burundi to an equal degree. We have to work on cultural curiosity. Students learning the language are interested in what makes English-language cultures work; the *Coca-Colanisation* of most of the world is a measure of how cultural features can be assimilated through marketing. In a sense, we are marketing imaginative exploration. But in no sense does this imply cultural imperialism. As we shall see later, there can be many kinds of reason for studying English literature, but *studying* is a rather different aspect of the question. It indicates a specialisation in the subject or the discipline of literary studies, which is a long way away from the exploitation of an incidental interest in the content of imaginative production (which may or may not be literary). The difference is fundamentally between literary materials as a *means* and as an *end*.

Imaginative stimuli of various kinds constitute the basis of this approach. An evaluation of the usefulness of any item has to take into consideration some or all of the features which follow.

To succeed, as Sperber and Wilson concisely put it (1986:155), 'an act of ostensive communication must attract the audience's attention.' 'Attention' is, in fact, more important here than 'interest', for, as we said earlier, there is no subject that will be intrinsically interesting to every learner of English. So, what is done *with* the text to make it draw, and hold, the reader's attention is every bit as vital as the content of the text itself.

Relevance and recognition

Identification transfer at its very simplest involves the recognition by the reader of the fact that the words on the page are not purely referential, not to be taken absolutely literally, but that they have some relevance to an overall frame of discourse, to a wider-ranging subject-matter, and indeed may even have intertextual relationships with other pieces of written (or other) discourse which may or may not be familiar to the reader.

Relevance is a key word here, and, as Sperber and Wilson convincingly show, a key concept in all communication. To what is the text relevant? It should in some way be relevant to the student, whatever other relevancies it may have. If the text is an extract, how much of its relevance to the text that originally surrounded it has been lost or betrayed in the process of extrapolation? Is the text's relevance to other texts the students may be reading or already have read more important than the integrity of the whole original text? Is the context given or chosen, imposed or open?

These, and a host of similar questions, could be debated endlessly, and cannot conveniently be set aside for purely pragmatic reasons. We will find ourselves constantly returning to them as we proceed with our evaluation of texts and discussion of criteria of text selection.

Let us take the word *relevance* as our starting point. A reader will decide fairly quickly whether a text is relevant to his or her interests, whether it coincides with his or her assumptions, and whether or not it can be processed to advantage.

The context in which the piece of text is read, or at least approached, is important. Obviously, a learner should be able to trust his or her teacher sufficiently to assume that the text given will be accessible; that is, that it will not present too many difficulties in terms of the level of language knowledge required, or in relation to the level of knowledge of the world, for that particular student or class.

To give an absurd example, no teacher would give a class of fourteen year-old intermediate students of English a dissertation on nuclear physics, or, indeed, *The Canterbury Tales* in the original Middle English.

But it is precisely here that problems begin. I have, in my own experience, encountered teaching situations where Chaucer and *Starting Strategies* were being taught to the same learners—a situation many may believe is impossible, but one which pertains in academic institutions in several countries. What might be called the relevance gap is, in that kind of situation, enormous. Relevance has to cover linguistic capability, as well as curriculum value and inherent interest. Taking such a situation as an undesirable extreme, I want to show how the relevance gap, present in almost any L2 representational context, can successfully be bridged and overcome.

The idea that literature is not 'relevant' to learners is easily quashed. Natural curiosity about the world, and about any text to be read, means that a learner is always willing to make some attempt to bridge the relevance gap which the teacher may fear separates the learner and the text.

Relevance is not purely dependent on content. Nor is the vague quality of 'literariness' *ir*relevant to learners' experience. Recognition plays a considerable part in making reading relevant to the reader. Being able to recognise references, contexts, allusions, and so on, adds to the breadth of the reading experience. So it is not necessary to try to avoid what may seem, at first sight, not to be immediately relevant to the particular learning situation.

The relevance gap is bridged by identification of (if not necessarily *with*) different ways of seeing the world, and the range of ways of expressing such a vision.

7   IMAGINATION AND INVOLVEMENT

Ways of seeing/ways of saying

THE INDIVIDUAL VIEWPOINT OF A WRITER, photographer, or any other artist communicating a message is what must reach the individual reader. Often in imaginative expression, especially written, the representational language used is figurative. It is part of the nature of representational language that it be so; indeed, deconstructionist theory—which opens up infinite possibilities in the 'free play' of meanings—would maintain that the boundaries between literary and other kinds of discourse are dissolved. All language, at that point, becomes figurative.

This is, in a limited sense, an attractive theory, but it has become obfuscated by academicism. Unfortunately, perhaps, it has become part of the exegetical process that figurative expression has become overloaded with metalanguage and critical terminology. These have their place at a high academic level of discourse, but are largely irrelevant, discouraging, and confusing to the L2 learner.

As so often, the teacher has to distil from the Olympian heights of theoretical exposition the necessary practical applications to a classroom situation. The teacher must facilitate and encourage the learning process, and this requires a clear, unclouded understanding of terminology and concepts as they relate to a particular teaching and learning situation. Two quotations might serve as warnings to the over-enthusiastic teacher:

A little learning is a dangerous thing. (*Alexander Pope*)

and Terry Eagleton's timely:

Trying to combine structuralism, phenomenology and psychoanalysis is more likely to lead to a nervous breakdown than to a brilliant literary career. (1983; quoted in *Wales*, 1989:358)

These should keep language teachers at a safe distance from the mystification of literary linguistics. But it is to be hoped that the warning does not put them off the basic application of a representational methodology.

It is not necessary for students to be aware of very much more than a few basic concepts of representational language use: metaphor and metonymy, polysemy, parallelism, euphemism, rhyme and rhythm, assonance and alliteration cover most of the likely requirements of non-specialist students.

And it is not even necessary that they actually learn these terms as such. Recognition is the first step towards familiarity. When a similar effect has been encountered twice or three times, and reference made back to the earlier experiences, students develop a capacity for actively identifying the effect—and thence, if they wish, they can proceed to give it a name, and will be happy to do so.

It can be demotivating and counterproductive to present critical terminology and metalanguage prior to exemplification; conversely, it can be both rewarding and stimulating for students to be able to put a name to an effect once they have seen what the effect is and something of how it is achieved.

Despite the risk of contradicting what I have just said, it may be useful to examine very briefly the examples of terminology mentioned above.

Metaphor and **metonymy**, two of the mainstays of imaginative representation, involve a transfer of identity, in a rather similar way to the educational use of cartoon characters; without any overt didactic intent, of course. Metaphor and metonymy transfer the literal sense of a phrase to another level on which the reader/receiver understands the message at a remove from the basic literal sense.

The word *metaphor* comes from Greek, and literally means 'carrying from one place to another.' It indicates an implicit comparison (as opposed to a *simile*, which is explicit, and is usually introduced in English by *like* or *as*); flowers often provide a metaphor for love, for beauty, or for youth; rivers a metaphor for passing time; trees a metaphor for stability and growth.

The possibilities of metaphor are endless, and imaginative writing constantly explores and extends these possibilities. Almost any imaginative text will contain a network of such associations which the reader can explore, decode, interpret, and appropriate, according to his or her individual reactions and responses.

Let us take a famous line of English poetry as an example:

What passing-bells for these who die as cattle?

This is the first line of Wilfred Owen's First World War sonnet, 'Anthem for Doomed Youth'. It is not an easy line for an L2 learner to decode, and this is largely due to the denseness of its figurative language—its use of metaphor and metonymy. A highly sophisticated reader could give a lengthy exposition of the allusive qualities inherent even in the title. But in the present context, we do not want to aim too high. Suffice it to say that the line quoted contains a metaphor of death and burial in 'passing-bells', and, with 'as', a simile for meaningless mass slaughter. The rhetorical question form opens up the whole area of the questioning of war and human destruction that the poet is writing about.

The reader accepts this use of metaphor and the widespread use of figurative language without necessarily identifying all the devices as such—it is assimilated as part of the text's communicative function. Metaphor is the flesh of imaginative writing, words (lexis and syntax) the bones on which the flesh grows.

We could reduce the Owen line to a very basic summary: 'A lot of men died, and were buried without a proper funeral.' The basic information is conveyed in referential language—that is, without imagery or, indeed, any level of emotional involvement on the part of reader or writer. When we add the simile 'as cattle', there is already the beginning of a move away from the merely referential; the choice of the simile indicates something of the speaker's attitude to the carnage. That is fundamental. Attitude, or the adoption of a stance in relation to what is being described, is one of the most vital factors which contribute to the interactive possibilities of a text. And the choice of figurative expression is one of the first moves away from the bald communication of information in a referential form.

Metonymy is, in a sense, simpler. It transfers indexically the identity of a thing to a limited example of that thing: 'the Crown' stands for the monarchy, for example, and 'the stage' stands for the world of the theatre, 'the sea' for all aspects of sea-faring. There is, therefore, a direct or logical relationship of contiguity between the original referent and the word employed to stand for it. The transfer of identity is encoded by the writer (the producer of the message), and decoded by the reader (the receiver of the message) in the context of the overall communication.

Reading imaginative or ideational texts at any level requires the development in the reader of a capacity to decode such messages, such uses of metonymy and metaphor, moving away from the literal towards the figurative, in order to understand what the writer is trying to say.

Some writers, of course, are deliberately obscure and impenetrable, and introducing them and their work to readers unfamiliar with their codes would be foolhardy in the extreme. But most writers do want their words to be understood, to reach a readership which will accept, digest, and reflect on what they have read.

The use of such devices as metaphor is necessary: language has to be stretched, and very few messages are so simple that they can be rendered without some recourse to imagery. Similarly, few stories can be told in the present tense: the simple past is the most commonly used tense in narrative, but time-shifts have to be expressed, time itself may indeed be queried, the 'truths' narrated are variable, and their possible interpretations manifold.

The vital importance of metaphor and similar figurative techniques in differentiating representational from referential language is brought out in this strongly worded affirmation:

> The fear of metaphor and rhetoric in the empiricist tradition is a fear of subjectivism—a fear of emotion and the imagination. Words are viewed as having "proper senses" in terms of which truth can be expressed. To use words metaphorically is to use them in an improper sense, to stir the imagination and thereby the emotions and thus to lead us away from the truth and towards illusion.
>
> LAKOFF AND JOHNSON, 1980:191

The move 'away from the truth and towards illusion' is an important one, and is 'improper' only in that it invites the readers/participants to depart from the denotational limitations of the language they use. Emotional involvement is not a prerequisite, but imaginative involvement is. And once the imagination is engaged, some kind of subjective or emotional reaction begins to influence the ways of seeing of the participant.

Polysemy is the capacity of a word to have more than one meaning. Students do not necessarily have to know what polysemy is, but they will very quickly be able to recognise a pun when they see one. *Play* is one of the best examples of polysemy, having a range of meanings both as a verb and as a noun:

- (**v**) to move about lightly; to direct light or water; to engage in a pleasurable activity; to recite or rehearse; to go through a game; to participate in games; to perform; to compete... *(and more.)*
- (**n**) drama; an action (with a sword, for example); movement of light; recreative activity; procedure in a game... *(and more.)*

A pun (or paronomasia) occurs when a writer deliberately *plays* with polysemy, often in order to achieve a comic or otherwise striking effect. As such, it is widely used in advertising—one of the most elementary forms of linguistic manipulation by the producer of a message upon a receiver:

- Go to work on an egg (after *eating* an egg, rather than sitting on one!)
- You get a great deal from us (deal = business arrangement; a great deal = a lot)
- Travellin' style (travel in style)

The technique is also widely used in literature, perhaps most famously by Thomas Hood:

> *Ben Battle was a soldier bold,*
> *And used to war's alarms;*
> *A cannonball took off his legs,*
> *So he laid down his arms.*

These puns are not easy for the L2 learner to explain, but are not particularly difficult to assimilate—especially the Hood, where memory retention impact is reinforced by the rhythm and rhyme of the text. The key factor in the use of polysemy is *ambiguity*. The writer takes advantage of the possible multiplicity of meaning of the punning word, and it is up to the reader to receive the message —enjoying the ambiguity or not, as the case may be.

Nonsense words can be useful in this context, for the assumptions they evoke and the ambiguities they open up. Take, for example, the opening lines of Lewis Carroll's 'Jabberwocky':

> *'Twas brillig, and the slithy toves*
> *Did gyre and gimble in the wabe.*

L2 students will inevitably recognise or associate different nonsense words from those than an L1 reader would notice. 'Brillig' will be more recognisable for an L2 reader—who might associate it with *brilliant* (where an L1 speaker might think of the colloquial 'brill')—than 'toves' which, for an L1 speaker, might be associated with 'toads' or 'toes'.

Lodge (1988:30) refers to the Russian formalist Victor Shklovsky in analysing how nonsense words operate in this context: 'We create words with no referents or with ambiguous referents in order to force attention to the objects represented by the similar-sounding words. By making the reader go through the extra step of interpreting the nonsense word, the writer prevents an automatic response.'

The L2 reader is always a step or two behind the L1 reader in producing an 'automatic response'. This is because, in the first place, he or she has to decide if the unfamiliar word is simply a new or unknown word, or if it is in fact a nonsense word. There is, therefore, something of a risk in using nonsense words with L2 learners, unless they are primed to accept the possibility that some of the words they are reading are, strictly speaking, meaningless.

It is natural—and more obviously so in a language-learning context—for a reader to expect there to be a meaning to any text, especially if it is used in class. Human beings are conditioned to expect meaning. So deliberate absence of meaning has to be handled carefully, so that learners do not feel cheated or foolish. The question 'What does [the word] make you think of?' thus becomes vital in encouraging the student to open up mental areas of associative meaning potential when handling nonsense words. The technique can then very usefully be applied when handling unknown vocabulary which *does* have meaning.

Ambiguity in the case of a pun is lexical. It can also happen grammatically, where a structure can be open to more than one interpretation:

Dogs must be carried on escalators.

The receiver of this message who is dogless might feel trapped, unless the message is rapidly reassessed. The effect of ambiguity is, of course, not limited to the comic but, in an L2 situation, such comic examples of word-play are the most useful starting-point for students to find their way positively into the world of 'wordsplay'.

Taking this a step further, we come to ambivalence or equivocation, where a serious use of more than one meaning possibility is intended, as in this famous line from the opening scene of *Macbeth*:

Fair is foul and foul is fair.

Here, everything to do with good/bad, positive/negative is deliberately rendered equivocal, and the theme will be extensively developed through the play. As Tom Stoppard put it in a more recent example (still theatrical in context), 'An exit from some place is an entrance somewhere else.' If students are not trained to tune in to this kind of thinking, a great deal of the potential enjoyment of representational materials will be missed.

The uses of metaphor, or of ambiguity, imply a process of defamiliarisation. The expression of the familiar by the unfamiliar, the bringing together of the expected and the unexpected, creates an interactive participatory area between receiver and text—and it is in this area that *interpretation* begins. Meaning constructs in this area have to go beyond the referential. Denotational meanings are called into question, connotations are explored, reality is questioned, and judgement passes to the reader.

Parallelism is one of the simplest and most common devices, usually depending on repetition, as in 'He came, he saw, he conquered.' It has been described as 'foregrounded regularity' and, as such, can be easily identified by readers. Phonological effects, such as assonance and alliteration (repetition of the same stressed vowel and repetition of the initial consonant, respectively), often underscore an effect of parallelism.

Alliteration

- *Round and round the rugged rock the ragged rascal ran.* ('r' sounds)
- *Tramp, tramp, tramp, the boys are marching.* ('tr' and 'm' sounds)

Assonance

- *Round and round the spicy downs the yellow Lotos-dust is blown.*
  ('aʊ' and 'əʊ' sounds)

Assonance and alliteration are often found together, as in the following examples. Often an **onomatapoeic** effect is created, to bring out the sounds:

The murmurous haunt of flies on summer eves. (*'m' sounds as well as 's' and '3:' sounds*)

Break, break, break,
On thy cold gray stones, O Sea!
(*'br' sounds as well as 'el' and ' əʊ' sounds*)
Wailing, wailing, wailing, the wind over land and sea.
(*'w' and 'nd' sounds and, again, repeated words*)

Sounds and sense go closely together here, as often happens with representational materials in any context, from advertising slogans to epic poetry. When rhythm and rhyme are brought in, the effects are enhanced, as in

Soothed with the sound, the king grew vain,
Fought all his battles over again.
(smooth 's' sounds as well as rhyming: '-ain')

Rhyme is not indispensable to a successful effect of parallelism in poetry, as can be seen in:

Passing the visions, passing the night,
Passing, unloosing the hold of my comrades' hands,

Passing the song of the hermit bird and the tallying song of my soul,
Victorious song, death's outlet song, yet varying, ever-altering song.

Here, 'passing' creates the 'foregrounded regularity'; and the repeated 'song', alliterating with 'soul', creates the overall musical effect.

So far, we have been studying effect rather than meaning, and this might be challenged as unproductive in language-teaching terms. It is, however, indispensable as part of the development of students' language awareness, in finding out both what words can do and what can be done with words.

Language teaching can easily remain caught in a meaning trap: the assumption that everything has a meaning, and that understanding the meaning will make 'everything' clear. This is patently false.

But the affective trap can be just as risky in its way: we must beware of only evaluating or explaining representational texts in terms of the emotional (or physical) responses they stimulate in the reader—the 'affective fallacy', as it has been called. Affective approaches are an immensely useful starting-point for L2 students in moving from referential to representational materials. But *no* approach is a be-all and end-all. If overdone, the affective approach can become sentimental and self-indulgent; a certain objective distance may be kept as long as the teacher has clear didactic aims and objectives in mind.

I have left **euphemism** till last, since it begs the very important question of lexical choice. The word comes from Greek, as do so many words in this context, and means, literally, 'speak well'. Euphemism occurs a great deal in English when an inoffensive or indirect word is used in order to avoid a harsh, over-explicit or taboo word. Death being a socially taboo subject, the verb 'to die' is often replaced by 'to pass away', 'to pass on', and a host of similar expressions (parodied by television's *Monty Python's Flying*

Circus, with its memorable climax, 'rung down the curtain and joined the choir invisible').

The phenomenon is not peculiar to English. It is common to most languages and is therefore immensely useful in helping students to understand and evaluate lexical choice: why one expression is preferred to another. This opens up areas of social discourse, of politeness strategies, of register, of displacement (or 'deconstructionist deferral'), all of which in some way have to do with the *avoidance* of too directly explicit a meaning.

'When I see a spade I call it a spade,' says Cecily, in Oscar Wilde's *The Importance of Being Earnest;* only to be answered by Gwendolen's 'I am glad to say that I have never seen a spade.' Calling a spade a spade is a proverbial justification for bluntness, for not mincing one's words. But social constraints frequently compel a degree of lexical substitution in order to achieve one's aims, not to offend, to hide one's true feelings, and so on. This is where teacher discretion is advised at all times.

In teaching terms, the possibilities of linguistic concealment and revelation are rich. Obviously, the teacher has to employ a certain amount of discretion in terms of taboo areas (sex, defecation, religion, death) and bad language (although students are usually very quick on the uptake here, and usually fairly discreet themselves in not wishing to go too far in the teacher's presence).

As always, it will be the teacher's authority and the clarity of teaching objectives which will make the exploration of lexical choice a crucial step forward in language learning. Because, from an understanding of *why* certain lexical choices have been made, students can evaluate the actual words chosen, and *how* the message has been conveyed. The concept of addresser/addressee is important here, as is the question of register. For instance, it is exceedingly difficult for an L2 student to identify the precise discourse situation here:

Would you just slip out of that blouse a moment, my dear.

Awareness of register allows a native speaker to place this as male doctor/ female patient discourse, with an older/younger component to it as well. Such register identification is at the upper extremes of L2 learning, and most students would not be interested in aiming so high. But identification of *who* might be speaking, and *to whom,* can be very instructive in helping students to become aware of register and its concomitant questions of lexical choice. Register can be well-dressed language, or language dressed in an old T-shirt, jeans and trainers. This analogy may be more accessible to students than 'a variety of language defined according to the situation'; although this definition will become valuable when students have acquired some familiarity with the concept of register.

For example, students will both enjoy and learn from trying to decide who might be addressing whom in these texts.

1. *Don't congregate on the stairs, boy.*
2. *Christ, man! Didn't someone ever tell you that if you've got a few suspicious circumstances you're expected to hold on to a few of the suspects?*
3. *One turns to me his appealing eyes—poor boy! I never knew you, Yet I think I could not refuse this moment to die for you, if that would save you.*
4. *Where do you think you're going at this time of night?*
5. *You fucking nicked, me old beauty.*
6. *We are fighting, as we have always fought, for the weak as well as the strong. We are fighting for great and good causes.*
7. *Oh, just half a pint, thanks.*
8. *To the first of your questions the answer is in the affirmative.*
9. *I couldn't do it as cheap as I'd like, sir.*
10. *We're not in love all over again, and you know it.*

It is important to stress at the outset that, in this kind of exercise, there are no 100% right or wrong answers. It is not a guessing game; more an awareness-building experiment in working out the possible circumstances of each utterance and relating them to the possible interlocutors. Students, if encouraged to use their imaginations—although they should always justify their answers by close reference to the texts—should come up with a series of responses which will have brought cognitive learning, personal experience, linguistic knowledge, cultural awareness, and classroom interaction into play.

Have we lost sight of euphemism? Not at all—as numbers five (distinctly uneuphemistic) and eight in particular show. The subject can be taken further if we bring in 'government-speak', advertising language, and similar varieties of language. In government-speak, for instance, 'deterrent' can be a standard euphemism for 'missile' or 'bomb', and a 'rodent operative' is in fact a rat-catcher. Geoffrey Leech calls this (and the related phenomenon in advertising) 'associative engineering'. Readers *have* to read between the lines of an advertisement which speaks of 'a bijou garden flat, in need of some redecoration.' The truth is probably a tiny, crumbling basement.

This is learning to read the world, if the term is not too presumptuous. Students develop a capacity to make judgements, to evaluate and to select, which begins to take them beyond a merely subjective response to what they read.

Helping readers, especially in a foreign language, into this world of representational language and its effects is rather like Alice's falling down the rabbit-hole in *Alice's Adventures in Wonderland*. The 'rules' of language learning have to be bent a little; the accepted norms of level, or register, and of communication must be questioned. It does not, however, take long for students to accept the principles of representational language: the first principle, that the words on the page *stand for* something rather than literally *mean* something, is fundamental to representation in all cultures. There is no tribe on earth so wretched that it does not express its aspirations and dreams in stories, tales, poems, and songs.

The process of educating learners in the representational use of language is one of familiarisation. It is not to be rushed. It must be closely linked to the learning of referential language and of the syntactic mechanisms of the target language; for only in that way can any comparative sense of language use be developed. Representational language, as we have said, breaks the 'rules' of grammar, of word order, and so on. The learner can only understand how these rules are being broken if he or she has some familiarity with the rules themselves. But rules, as they say, are made to be broken.

As David Birch has persuasively put it (1988:158), 'as readers we are able to recognize the ambiguity choices which we, as people with stylistic competences, have constructed. That in turn requires of us a skill with language; a skill with grammatical structures; a skill with words; a skill with meanings. [...] That...is surely the securest way we have of beginning the interpretative process; the most articulate way we have of trying to understand and explain why we read something in the way we do—why we react in a particular way.' Birch is talking about readers who 'have constructed' their reading and stylistic competences. But his words must echo down the corridors of language-teaching establishments around the world, since they bring out forcibly the *necessity* of ambiguity in texts, and in readers' relationships with texts.

Gunther Kress (1988:141) takes the argument into the social sphere: 'texts are always and everywhere enmeshed in the social relations of writers and readers, and in their relations with social structures. It is that dynamic which gives rise to what we call style in text, and it is that dynamic which ensures that language is everywhere a part of social life.'

Frames of reference

Clearly, referential language is bounded by the frame of reference of the discourse involved. A word in isolation—'cat' or 'dog', for example—needs some contextual referent in order both to limit and clarify its meaning. 'Cat' can mean a domestic feline or a tiger, 'dog' anything from a chihuahua to the Hound of the Baskervilles, and both can be used in a personalised way, with some kind of insulting intention.

But a word can stand alone and imply its referents.

'Dog,' he said.
She closed the door.

The single word uttered has been enough for both interlocutors successfully to communicate and to arrive at an action. Anyone who is not party to the discourse will not know *(a)* whether the dog is left outside or shut in, *(b)* whether 'Dog' was a warning, a succinct communication of information, or a pre-established code-word with no canine referent at all.

It is very difficult for communication to take place without reference. (See Carter, 1987:14-16.) A shared frame of reference allows interlocutors to communicate without lengthy explanation.

'Lousy game.'
'Should have been ours.'
'Referee was blind.'
'Mm. It was a goal.'

This exchange has to be filled out by any non-participant in order to decode the overall content, and thus the meaning. Students learning English as a second language will not find it easy to penetrate such an exchange, but key words like 'game', 'referee' and 'goal' contextualise it sufficiently for understanding to be reached. This involves the student bringing knowledge of the world—in this case, of sport (probably football)—to bear on the text.

If the sport is unfamiliar, the decoding exercise will be considerably more difficult.

'Lousy rubber.'

or *'Trouble with my mallet.'*

or *'The lie of the green.'*

These utterances create technical difficulties simply because the reader/ student is often unfamiliar with the technical terminology of the particular sport under discussion.

Specialised language can be clarified by narrative explication.

> After the final of the golf championship, he was asked why he missed the final hole. 'The lie of the green,' he replied.

Perhaps only golfers would understand the fuller implications, but the reader would at least be able to contextualise the previously unreferenced 'the lie of the green'.

A significant part of the teacher's role in the use of representational materials is contextual. In the selection of materials, the first thing which must be clear is a context, either within the text itself or in the presentation of the text to be handled. A few examples will show how some kind of context is communicated, even in very short texts.

> Daphne, Alice thought, had missed her vocation. She would have made a startling impact on filmgoers as a kind of female Boris Karloff.

∾

She was fond of her children in an uneven, impulsive way. She would sometimes gather them passionately to her heart; she would sometimes forget them.

~

Jean stayed with her, trying to reassure her that Tessa wouldn't go off with some sinister man in a car, but that if such a man approached her, she might be scared and run away.

~

There was nothing but to sit still, tormented by maddening regret. I pictured what would be transpiring at Caddagat now; what we had done this time last week, and so on, till the thing became an agony to me.

~

It was Mr Knox who talked, but it was Uncle Stephen who provided subjects. It was like that game in which you scribble a line on a piece of paper and the other person fills it in, making it a horse or a man or a car or a boat. Tom, as usual, saw it like this, in a picture.

~

In the far distance, a helicopter skimmed down between the roofs, hovered for an instant like a bluebottle, and darted away again with a curving flight.

~

Jean turned the leaves back, showing other pages, the text varied here and there by capital letters and things written in red, then set the book back as it had been, when Crimond had finished writing that morning. It was like being shown a holy manuscript or rare work of art, something to be marvelled at, not, by the uninitiated, actually studied.

~

The Nile, at night, is jewelled. The bridges wear necklaces of coloured lights; all along the banks the houseboats are ablaze, festooned with gold, glowing against the dark swirling patterned water. One of these houseboats is a night-club; it throbs with music into the small hours.

~

But Benjamin did not cry. He simply pursed his mouth and turned his sad grey eyes on his brother. For it was Lewis, not he, who was whimpering with pain, and stroking his own left hand as if it were a wounded bird.

~

Monet would have made a pretty good job of us, thought Cuckoo, just as we are now. Two ladies sitting in the dappled shade of an apple-tree, a drift of poppies, green summer grasses, a high clump of valerian: me in my old straw hat, Leni bare-legged, the sun spilling over her white blouse like a scattering of sovereigns.

These short passages tell the reader something clear and identifiable about character, or about a place, or about something which has happened. Each gives a reference to someone or something outside the narrative context, in order to give the reader a better idea of the person or place described.

The referents here are used to represent some distinctive feature of the character or location. The reader has to make the mental leap, shift the frame of reference from the descriptive to the imagined or remembered, in order to complete the effect. 'Piece out our imperfections with your thoughts,' exhorted the Chorus in Shakespeare's *Henry the Fifth*. Here the 'imperfections' are deliberate. They are invitations to the reader to participate in the descriptive process. 'As' and 'like' feature strongly in this kind of imagination transfer: any simile or metaphor depends to a greater or lesser extent on the reader's capacity to recognise its frame of reference. The expansion of a simple description into figurative language, or a wider frame of reference, implies the reader's willing imaginative participation in the communicative act.

In teaching terms, students have to be enabled to recognise, and wherever possible identify, such narrative moves and techniques. A question like, 'What can you tell about Daphne (or Alice!)?' or, 'What is the mother's relationship with her children, in your opinion?' takes the process a vital step further. The reader is invited to reflect, to participate affectively, to judge. And in this, personal reactions, attitudes and experience will play a very significant part. The writer presupposes familiarity with cultural referents—from Monet to Boris Karloff—and trusts that the reader who sees the Nile as 'jewelled' will call up a mental picture as positive in the receiver's mind as it was in the producer's. 'How can a helicopter be "like" a bluebottle?' invites the student to evaluate the positive or negative intention behind the author's use of the image.

Such a range of cultural reference, taken to extremes, can discourage a reader considerably. Simpler metaphors, lower-order comparisons, make for easier identification; a complete character can be summed up in an extended simile, as in this example from Dickens' *David Copperfield*.

> It was Miss Murdstone who was arrived, and a gloomy-looking lady she was; dark, like her brother, whom she greatly resembled in face and voice; and with very heavy eyebrows, nearly meeting over her large nose, as if, being disabled by the wrongs of her sex from wearing whiskers, she had carried them to that account. She brought with her two uncompromising hard black boxes, with her initials on the lids in hard brass nails. When she paid the coachman she took her money out of a hard steel purse, and she kept the purse in a very jail of a bag which hung upon her arm by a heavy chain, and shut up like a bite. I had never, at that time, seen such a metallic lady altogether as Miss Murdstone was.

This is highly representational use of language. The conclusive adjective 'metallic' is the climax of an association of ideas (person/metal) which creates the character as she is seen by the first-person narrator. The effect is that the reader shares the narrator's negative view of Miss Murdstone, for two distinct but related reasons. First, all the associations are negative; and second, the narrator is in a privileged position vis-à-vis the reader and can impose his point of view on him/her. Very few readers will feel any sympathy with Miss Murdstone. To this extent, the negative description is highly partial. It is, indeed, a blatant manipulation of the reader's sympathy, both *for* the narrator and *against* the character described.

A question such as 'Are we intended to like the character?' can raise student awareness to this kind of manipulation of the reader's reaction, and lead to the first recognition of how imaginative writing very frequently sets up reader expectations and responses in order to achieve a particular aim.

Clearly this can be expanded enormously—but we are not engaged in literary criticism, simply in encouraging reader awareness as to how discourses can be manipulated and reader complicity created. For the reader must, to a certain extent, become something of an accomplice in the reading process if any effect is to be allowed. The reader is free to accept or reject any effects the writer tries to create; the first step is recognition of the fact that this is happening.

Imaginative involvement

Elementary imaginative engagement must arouse curiosity or stimulate a reaction (puzzlement, laughter, a wish to find out more, even a wish to avoid involvement) and, in doing so, it opens up interactive possibilities. A text that provokes no reaction, or that makes too many demands on the receiver, is counterproductive in learning terms. Elements which might suggest whether a text is making too many demands include: vocabulary; cultural awareness (or lack of it); beliefs (religious or otherwise); taboo areas; outrageousness; philosophical inapproachability.

No learner lives in a vacuum; we are all constantly exposed to 'difficult' concepts. And any teacher who knows his or her class will know how far it is possible to go in any of the above-mentioned risk areas. Religion, sex and money are often the key areas of cultural difference between English and other languages and have, in consequence, to be handled with care, to avoid unwittingly giving offence. But this does not mean that representational materials have to be censored or sifted for high-risk content. Learners make some allowance for the host culture and its assumptions, just as good teachers will seek to accommodate learners' cultural backgrounds in their work.

What *is* to be avoided is imposition, or what used to be called 'cultural imperialism'. It has to be remembered at all times that the basic aim is to teach *language*. Clearly, culture is implicit in language, and any cultural context must reflect a series of assumptions—from the hegemonical to the ethical—which are part and parcel of the prevailing world view. Value judgements implicit in L1 cultural assumptions may be brought into question in an L2 learning context. This is all to the good. For if the learner is aware that he or she is not expected blindly to accept the cultural assumptions of the language being learned, he or she can then become more consciously selective in evaluating, recognising, accepting, and rejecting aspects of the society whose language he or she is learning.

Education should, at its best, be subversive. This does not mean the overthrow of values and standards, but the constant constructive questioning of assumptions, attitudes and standpoints. In the context of language learning and teaching, this awareness of what is being studied, what is being taught, and what is being learned (and these can be three distinct though closely related features) must lead to a questioning of language at all its levels.

- Language tells—but what?
- Language describes—but how? and how well?
- Language informs—but who? and how much?
- Language deceives.
- Language entertains.
- Language placates.
- Language arouses emotions.
- Language reveals.
- Language conceals.
- Language distorts.
- Language ...

The list is endless. Any language learner who is not made aware of these aspects of language is not learning *about* language; how it works, how it is used, and how the learner can—and should—be able to use it.

Culture and shock

Language is dangerous. The so-called communicative revolution, and its concomitant insistence on functions, has tended to emasculate language, reducing it to the sweet-tasting oil of international mutual comprehension. That this is valuable cannot be denied, but there is a danger that the communication achieved remains on a level that is conditioned by the referential nature of its functionality. I am not suggesting that language teachers should go out of their way to shock and provoke their students beyond the levels of communication, reflection, and discussion around which syllabuses and examinations are oriented. But polite levels of social intercourse have to be considered as only one area in the vast potential range of language deployment.

Some students wish to be protected from the violence that language can contain—and this is to be respected. The reality of living language cannot, however, be ducked; and seeing four-letter words painted on walls is both a confirmation of this and an affirmation of the necessity of language to communicate inner feelings, which might be difficult to articulate in a polite social context.

As Ronald Carter has said (1987:211), 'words contain and conceal ideology.' This fundamental factor relates closely to M. A. K. Halliday's view (1978) of language as social semiotic. Educators have to underline both how words *operate* and how they are *operated on* by those who use them. Take this example of language use, which would nowadays be considered unacceptable:

We paid five shillings apiece for a liqueur, found a table, and took notice of the show. It seemed to me a wholly rotten and funereal business. A nigger band, looking like monkeys in uniform, pounded out some kind of barbarous jingle, and sad faced marionettes moved to it.

The prejudice displayed here is blatant—a social and cultural reflection of the time of writing (1924), and of a kind of writer(narrator)/reader relationship which would find nothing remarkable in the words. Every age and culture has its prejudices, and it is easy to feel superior in the face of what is clearly outdated. But present-day prejudice is easy to find.

When he had burnt Guy's books and smashed Guy's face, he hadn't really been indulging an intense hatred of homosexuals. God knows, he'd encountered enough of them before without feeling the need to beat them up. It was the years of exclusion, his son's defiant banishing of his own father that he was trying to smash.

The problem here lies precisely in identifying the point of view of the character (see diagram on page 127 of this chapter). Extrapolated from its context, this passage is highly ambiguous. It could represent an intolerant character who (heaven knows) has kept his intolerance in check. The word 'really', however, allows doubt to creep in, as does the adjective 'intense'; they could be used to justify a reading whereby the 'he' described is prejudiced, and violently so.

In selecting materials for teaching purposes, teachers should not necessarily endeavour to keep prejudice out (either their own or the authors') but rather, should ensure that the point of view of the writer, narrator, or character(s) concerned is not uncomfortably ambivalent, or compromised and rendered confusing by an undue lack of context. Ambiguity is, however, inherent in human nature, and over-positive affirmation is just as worrying as explicit negative prejudice.

Again, it is learner awareness that is being developed. Representational language rarely deals in certainties, and is rarely so blatant in its expressions of prejudice as the examples cited above (both tempered later in the books concerned). But, since prejudice is always with us, it is worth remembering that it can be very well hidden, as well as astonishingly explicit.

Identification and point of view

The movement towards an understanding of the meaning potential of representational language is to be seen in three stages: words; meanings of single words; meanings of words in groups. This then leads to stories and their meanings, then to the forms used to tell the stories and the effect that form has on meaning.

> *O for a beaker full of the warm South.*

This line (Keats, 'Ode to a Nightingale', line 15) is quite astonishingly inaccessible to the 'innocent' reader who has no familiarity with metaphorical use of language. Even a normal series of 'wh-' questions of the type used with referential texts does not necessarily clarify the line. *Who is speaking? To whom? What does he/she want? Where are they?* etc. could lead to pretty unedifying answers. The speaker is presumably the poet, or a voice he represents. This reveals one of the first problems with representational or ideational texts: the question of identification. Here no speaker is directly identified, although the use of the vocative 'O' indicates a speech act of some kind.

Identification of the speaker or intended speaker can be easy. 'Call me Ishmael,' the opening sentence of Herman Melville's *Moby Dick*, introduces a first-person narrator by name (the tone in which Ishmael presents himself is worthy of discussion too, in terms of its directness, its authority, its brevity). But when Louis MacNeice does a similar thing in "Prayer Before Birth"—'I am not yet born; O hear me'—we are to imagine the speaker as an unborn child. Already, in the very basic fact of identifying the speaking voice of the text, the reader has to move into an imaginative context; the process of identification is thus an essential first step into the fictional world created by the author. If the reader cannot in some way identify a speaking voice—even an invisible, impersonal, third-person narrator—he or she is often at a complete loss as to how to proceed with the text.

The following diagram may be useful in indicating the most common points of view in narrative writing (from McRae and Pantaleoni, 1985/1986:8).

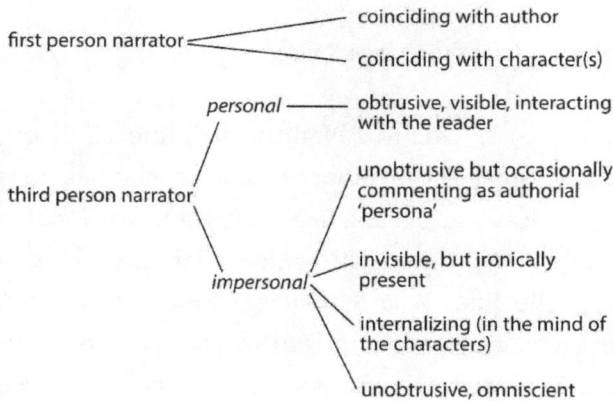

first person narrator — coinciding with author
— coinciding with character(s)

personal —— obtrusive, visible, interacting with the reader

third person narrator

unobtrusive but occasionally commenting as authorial 'persona'

invisible, but ironically present

impersonal

internalizing (in the mind of the characters)

unobtrusive, omniscient

The question of identification should not, however, be considered as some kind of riddle. 'Who am I?' is rarely the point, except in children's games. In selecting a text for class use, the teacher has to bear in mind that identification of the speaker (and, indeed, of all the participants in the action) should not be a tortuous process. If the speaker's identity is ambiguous, this should reflect the author's intention. Otherwise, the preliminary apparatus should clarify any possible ambiguity, unless that ambiguity is directly relevant to what the students will do with the text.

Immediately related to identification of the fictional or narratorial voice is the creation of that persona's fictional world: the reader has to work out now something about *where* the speaker is located. In the line of Keats quoted above, the speaker is probably not in the South. This is almost the only hypothesis a reader can come up with in the absence of further information from the speaker, and even then it would have to await confirmation or refutation later in the text.

What else can we look for in just one line? I suggest that one of the most important things this particular line reveals is 'attitude'. The speaker feels positive about the South—perhaps because it is warm—and wants a beaker of it. Positive or negative attitudes in the speaker's way of talking about, describing or evoking the subject matter of a text are among the very first things a reader can begin to intuit. These early intuitions may or may not be confirmed in later reading, but that does not deny their value.

Of course, reading one line is hardly a stimulating exercise, but it can occasionally prove fruitful. The present example would, I suggest, not be particularly useful to a class of L2 students unless they had some familiarity with the aspects of poetic discourse which are emerging in our discussion of it.

'What does "the... South" mean?' might be our next question; and here a host of implications come into play. A reader who knows absolutely nothing about the line or the poem it is taken from (never mind the writer), but who may be able to work out the basic meaning of the words, is now faced with 'a beaker' (normally containing liquids) and 'the... South' (normally a geographical indicator). The two can go together only if 'the... South' stands for something liquid.

The reader who lives in the southern hemisphere (Patagonia might be the extreme example) might find 'warm' a rather disorienting adjective. The line has to be seen as the expression of someone for whom the South *represents* something liquid, and also warmth; the association of sun and wine with the South is particular to Northern climates and consciousness.

A student from an Arab culture may find difficulty in understanding why wine should be desirable to the speaker. A student from a Mediterranean country might find sun and wine too normal to occasion such desire.

As soon as the metonymy of the South is used, it opens up the range of associations, contexts and frames of reference that make this line clearly English, in terms of both geography and sensibility. We could go on to: What does he like about the South? Is the South different? In short, from this point onwards, an almost endless series of hypothetical discussion possibilities is opened up, purely on the basis of the metonymy of South=wine.

Can our students be expected to go painstakingly through all the steps we have just gone through with every line they read? To pursue these points too closely would be both to kill the effectiveness of the line and to bore the students to distraction. But the example serves to show both how complex and how rich the meaning potential of one line can be.

It goes without saying that the later lines of the poem will amplify and extend the range of reference found in this first line. But what interests us here is how the teacher can use this awareness of the processes at work in the text to interest students in the text and what it is saying.

Expectation

When Alice, for example, encounters an 'enormous puppy', a whole range of expectations is brought into play. The *expectation gap* (the mental and associative area the reader brings to reading) is the productive area of many simple, and more complex, reading effects.

A puppy is usually small. 'Enormous' and 'puppy' are words that do not normally go together. The author, by using an unexpected collocation, wants to surprise the reader, to play with reader expectation. The scene in the novel is when Alice has eaten the cakes which have made her smaller; with the result that even a perfectly friendly little puppy seems enormous to her. The unexpected collocation surprises the reader into a closer realisation of Alice's point of view. The teacher can use this single conceit as the *point of entry* for a reading of a longer passage, which can be of any length, from one paragraph to eight.

Alice called out as loud as she could, 'If you do, I'll set Dinah at you!'

There was a dead silence instantly, and Alice thought to herself, 'I wonder what they *will* do next! If they had any sense, they'd take the roof off.' After a minute or two, they began moving about again, and Alice heard the Rabbit say, 'A barrowful will do, to begin with.'

'A barrowful of *what?*' thought Alice; but she had not long to doubt, for the next moment a shower of little pebbles came rattling in at the window, and some of them hit her in the face. 'I'll put a stop to this,' she said to herself, and shouted out, 'You'd better not do that again!' which produced another dead silence.

Alice noticed with some surprise that the pebbles were all turning into little cakes as they lay on the floor, and a bright idea came into her head. 'If I eat one of these cakes,' she thought, 'it's sure to make some change in my size; and, as it can't possibly make me larger, it must make me smaller, I suppose.'

So she swallowed one of the cakes, and was delighted to find that she began shrinking directly. As soon as she was small enough to get through the door, she ran out of the house, and found quite a crowd of little animals and birds waiting outside. The poor little lizard, Bill, was in the middle, being held up by two guinea-pigs, who were giving it something out of a bottle. They all made a rush at Alice the moment she appeared; but she ran off as hard as she could, and soon found herself safe in a thick wood.

'The first thing I've got to do,' said Alice to herself, as she wandered about in the wood, 'is to grow to my right size again; and the second thing is to find my way into that lovely garden. I think that will be the best plan.'

It sounded an excellent plan, no doubt, and very neatly and simply arranged; the only difficulty was, that she had not the smallest idea how to set about it; and while she was peering about anxiously among the trees, a little sharp bark just over her head made her look up in a great hurry.

An enormous puppy was looking down at her with large round eyes, and feebly stretching out one paw, trying to touch her. 'Poor little thing!' said Alice, in a coaxing tone, and she tried hard to whistle to it; but she was terribly frightened all the time at the thought that it might be hungry, in which case it would be very likely to eat her up in spite of all her coaxing.

The best beginning for this reading, if the teacher does not want to use the whole extract, will be the direct speech: 'If I eat one of these cakes. . .' This leaves the shrinking scene in its entirety, which leads to the size relationship with the 'enormous puppy', which was the starting-point.

The choice of such a point of entry to any reading can be immensely motivating to the students, especially if there is an expectation-gap effect which can be exploited. Naturally, the effect can come at any stage in the text and can be foregrounded as a pre-reading stimulus or as a linguistic effect.

Clearly, starting from a focal point in a longer text, even the turning point of the action, perhaps focuses reader attention on a chosen point of view in the text; it does not preclude alternative interpretation, although it may limit it. However, the point is more that the choice of focus indicates an approach to a text which can thereafter be applied to a wider range of texts; and, in this circumstance, interpretation possibilities are not impeded.

One of the most famous of such expectation-gap effects is the opening line of George Orwell's *Nineteen Eighty-Four:* 'It was a bright cold day in April, and the clocks were striking thirteen.' The effect is gained because clocks do not strike thirteen. But history has caught up with Orwell. In countries where the 24-hour clock is the norm, even educated, aware readers often do not notice the effect and have to be shown it. (And the effect is usually lost in translation too.)

Expectations are easily aroused. Any reader who is given a text expects it to mean something, and so looks for some kind of meaning. Expectations come into play largely at the connotational level. Let us take Alice's puppy as a starting-point.

'Puppy'—at the connotational level—means much more than its denotational meaning, 'a small young dog'. It evokes affective notions, and gives the reader an attitude to the animal. But any reader who has a phobia about dogs will have a completely different reaction and range of expectations!

The puppy is a dog. If a writer were to write simply

Dog

the reader would have complete liberty to imagine any dog, of any size, shape, age, colour, or temperament.

Black dog

would exclude a large majority of previously imagined canines.

Huge black dog

continues to eliminate reader choice, and begins to introduce an element of atmospheric tension. Many readers will start thinking of such references as *The Hound of the Baskervilles*—quite different from the enormous, but basically not-too-threatening, puppy.

A huge black dog with slavering jaws

compounds the atmosphere expectation.

A huge black dog with slavering jaws and only three legs…

reduces the poor hound a little. And if the sentence is completed as

… was waiting for a tram.

reader expectation has been built up only to be defeated—turned to a laugh, a damp squib.

Students enjoy being made aware of this process of expectation build-up, climax and effect; and it quickly becomes part of their reading competence to recognise how their expectations are being manipulated and, later, why.

An expectation gap is fundamental to many humorous effects, as well as to the kind of surprise effect Orwell created. The statement, 'I've got very sore misgivings,' seems to imply worry. An answer which demolishes that expectation creates humour: 'Put some talcum powder on them.'

A similar expectation-gap effect, as in the following example, is known as rank shift:

- *He opened the door in his pyjamas.*
- *What a strange place to have a door!*

L2 students are capable of grasping the basics of this kind of wordplay (and can relate it to their own language) if it is presented simply and in easily assimilated doses. More than two or three examples can defeat the whole exercise, and turn it into a show-off joke-telling session on the part of the teacher—at which most of the students will simply switch off in bewilderment.

8 TEXTS

Sense in nonsense

THERE IS NO AGE OR LANGUAGE-LEVEL OBSTACLE TO imagination. It is often argued that imaginative materials are the province only of the more advanced learner. This is not so.

The young learner uses games and fictional characters in language learning from the very beginning—there is no reason authentic imaginative texts cannot be introduced also at this level. The nature of the texts may still be highly ludic—Edwin Morgan's "Chinese Cat" or "Siesta of a Hungarian Snake", or George Macbeth's "Pavane for an Unborn Infanta" are eminently suitable for ten-year-olds, as well as for older learners of any age who have been studying English for more than a couple of hours.

p m r k g n i a o u
p m r k g n i a o
p m r k n i a o
p m r n i a o
p m r i a o
p m i a o
m i a o
m a o

~

s sz sz SZ sz SZ sz ZS zs ZS zs zs z

~

AN-AN CHI-CHI
AN-AN CHI-CHI

CHI-CHI AN-AN

CHI-AN

CHI-AN CHI-AN CHI-AN CHI-AN CHI
AN-CHI AN-CHI AN-CHI AN

CHI-AN CHI-AN CHI-AN CHI-AN CHI
AN-CHI AN-CHI AN-CHI AN

CHI-AN

AN-CHI AN-CHI AN-CHI AN
AN-CHI AN-CHI AN-CHI AN

CHI-CHI
AN-AN CHI-CHI
AN-AN CHI-CHI

CHI-CHI AN-AN
CHI-CHI AN-AN

AN-AN

AN-AN AN-AN AN-AN AN-AN

CHI-CHI CHI-CHI CHI-CHI
CHI-CHI CHI-CHI CHI-CHI

CHI-CHI

AN-AN AN-AN
AN-AN AN-AN

AN-AN AN-AN
AN-AN AN-AN

AN-AN

CHI-CHI CHI-CHI
CHI-CHI CHI-CHI

CHI-CHI CHI-CHI
CHI-CHI CHI-CHI

CHI-CHI

The point about these three texts is that they do not contain any words. The title therefore becomes very important. So, if the title is withheld from the students, the first object of the exercise can lie in their inventing a title for the text. The Morgan texts lend themselves to shorter exploitation than the Macbeth—they show students the possibilities of letters which make sounds and pictures. This discovery is then taken a step further if the third text is presented without a title: students' own opinions as to what the text is about will afford the first opportunities for classroom discussion and interaction on a representational text. And the important lesson to be learnt is that *what the text represents, or is about, depends on the reader.* Students will suggest that the poem is about trains, war planes, animals, Chinese people, or whatever comes into their heads.

With the Macbeth text, it is vital to give students as much interpretative space as possible. Even the teacher reading the text aloud will *close* this very open text in some way, limiting the interpretative possibilities. If students find their own ways into and around the text, they will then be able to judge better the validity of the text as *story* (rather than as an open text) when they are given the (rather obscure) title, with its reference to Ravel's *Pavane pour une Infante Défunte.* The actual story—of two giant pandas, An-An and Chi-Chi, from Moscow and London Zoos, whose relationship came to nothing (see McRae and Pantaleoni, 1990:115)—may very well come as a disappointment after the initial open experimentation. An open text has been reduced to a closed text, by imposing a story and a title upon it.

This shows that what can be done with the text can be, in some cases, even more important than the text itself—especially in the very earliest stages of students' experience with representational materials.

How much of the discussion is in English does not actually matter very much in the earliest stages of this kind of work—the titles students give to the text must be in English, and they should then be encouraged to answer the question 'Why?' as much as they can regarding their own choice of title in English. The sense of discovery, the realisation that a poem can be fun, the encouragement to play with words in English, are all of fundamental psychological importance with learners of all ages.

'Shape' poems—like "Siesta of a Hungarian Snake"—in such forms as stars, circles, steps, wings, birds, etc., can become part of students' creative writing, especially with younger learners. (Carter and Long (1987: 66-70, 79-81) give examples of this technique.)

Of course, at any level, there arise complex questions of text selection, suitability and exploitation. But it is important for all language teachers to give some thought to the question of *when* to introduce imaginative interaction in L2 learning. Traditionalists will argue the later the better, but the above examples, which perhaps cover a single lesson, might serve to show that preconceptions of literature and language level can actually be an impediment to useful communicative learning!

Teachers have always to give their students something to communicate *about* as well as the language capability to communicate *with*. That this communication can start from the ludic is now perfectly acceptable. Adult students are often a little more inhibited about allowing their imagination free rein, but this first selection of texts, in making no linguistic demands on them, presents them with an encouraging lack of constraints in arriving at their responses. Adult reactions to these texts may be of laughter, and occasionally may be dismissive. But only when their reactions are developed into carefully directed responses will they realise that there is method behind the seeming madness of using 'meaningless' texts: meaning depends on the reader. This has to be emphasised with adult learners, and capitalised on in subsequent use of more meaning centred texts. For adults are not used to finding their own meanings in a text, accustomed as they often are to being guided (or simply told) by a teacher what the text is about. This element of discovery gives a new realm of freedom of expression to the learning situation, which is a vital encouragement to communication.

In the early stages, the more open to interpretation the text being used, the greater is the students' disinhibition in offering interpretations and meaning possibilities.

Open/closed texts

I would take issue with the critic Umberto Eco's classification of open and closed texts. Where he sees genre fiction (thrillers, romances, and the like) as closed, I would suggest they are open, in that they still invite imaginative engagement between reader and text—albeit within a limited series of conventions. Eco acknowledges that such texts can be misread (or aberrantly decoded, as he would have it) and, at that point, he says, they become open texts. But this presumes that there is such a thing as a definably *correct* reading—which, in the individual relationship of interaction between reader and text, is a contradiction in terms.

I prefer to see *any* imaginative text as open, any purely referential text as closed. This is highly reductive, I admit. A scientific paper, while presenting information, can engage the aware reader's imagination. But here, Eco's criteria for closed texts (a specific reader in a specific social context) clearly hold. The more open a text is to interpretation, the further it is removed from the closed areas of restricted discourse, limited reactions and functional responses. The more appeal it makes beyond purely conceptual meaning (propositional, referential or denotational; i.e. the 'dictionary definition' kind of meaning), the more a text is open to connotative meaning, with the consequent opening-up of associations, emotions, ideas and the range of such second-order meanings.

'A house is not a home,' goes the song. Let us look at the meanings involved. When 'house' means a building, erection or edifice for habitational purposes, it is simply referential. But 'home' evokes connotations of domesticity, warmth, security, perhaps even family, which go far beyond mere bricks and mortar. 'Home', even as a lexical item, has a wider range of interpretational possibilities than 'house', which can cover a broad range of referential building types but hardly the affective possibilities of 'home'. I would suggest that even the simplest words can be open or closed, according to the inherent representational possibilities.

This concept should be related to students' own language. Comparative study will reveal, for example, that the house/home relation is not repeated in many languages (French/Spanish/Italian), but holds good in others. Every language can show examples of such lexical 'openness'—and individuals often have their 'own' special words, with particularly open or closed connotational meanings.

This kind of comparative and, indeed, personal exploration of meaning potential is to be encouraged at all levels: from children, who play freely with words and their possibilities, to adults, who may not have realised how much their own word stock is conditioned by connotational influences. It is these connotational possibilities which can make even the shortest text an 'open' text.

Poetry

Many language teachers shy away from using poetry, perhaps largely because of unfamiliarity with the pleasure of poetry, and deeply-rooted feelings that poetry is Literature at its most literary. Students may feel much the same; with the result that poetry and language teaching seem quite simply not to go together.

Poetic diction, poetic licence, and the concept of the poet as a kind of seer, somewhat outside the real world, all contribute to the distancing of poetry from day-to-day reality, and consequently from referential language, in the 'average' mind. Clearly, a great deal of poetry is less accessible to L2 learners than other kinds of representational materials.

I want to take two examples of texts which cover a range of reading possibilities for poetry—a subject which is handled more extensively, and with considerable enthusiasm, in Maley and Moulding's *Poem to Poem* (1985), although their book is disappointingly targeted at more advanced learners.

The following text could be approached as a simple functional message:

This is just to say I have eaten the plums that were in the icebox and which you were probably saving for breakfast. Forgive me, they were delicious, so sweet and so cold.

If students are asked, as a pre-reading question, where the message could be found, what its function is, or who is sending it to whom, a whole range of possibilities will be found. The text is, at first sight, both a simple message and an open text: a note apologising, but going on to describe sensations of enjoyment. No speaker is identified, nor a setting, although 'icebox' is a precursor to the word 'fridge', so a kitchen is almost implied. Students find a lot to notice of this kind, until the teacher asks the seemingly irrelevant question, 'Is it a poem?' Clearly, as it stands, it does not *look* like a poem. This is the first step towards having students think about what their preconceptions of poetry involve. Form—or call it graphology, the look, the shape, whatever—is the first condition of a text being a poem for most students. They expect verses, if not also rhyme; and layout is at the heart of this expectation.

So, if the text is now presented as it was originally written, does it suddenly change from being 'not a poem' to being a poem?

This is Just to Say

I have eaten
the plums
that were in
the icebox

and which
you were probably
saving
for breakfast

Forgive me
they were delicious
so sweet
and so cold

The text does acquire more 'meaning' in this form and can be looked at from various points of view, ranging from line length or punctuation to roles and sensuality. The trick of asking students how the text would be different if a word were to be omitted is useful here: 'just' and 'so' are good words to examine in this way. And what title would students have given to the poem? Do they like the writer's trick of using the first line as title?

Poems by a range of writers, from William Carlos Williams (the author of this text), through early Ezra Pound, to Brian Patten and Roger McGough, can offer stimulating materials of this kind for use in the language classroom. Among the activities teachers can use are:

- reformulation as 'not a poem';
- keeping back the title;
- rewriting in different words or form;

- changing the speaker ('I found this note. . . ');
- re-forming lines and verses;
- omitting words or substituting them;
- playing with capital letters (as e e cummings does) and punctuation;
- identifying speaker, situation, and function;
- finding what makes the text a poem;
- finding levels of intention (message, sensual pleasure, etc.).

All this can be done before, or separately from, any thematic discussion that the text might stimulate. So a range of levels of involvement is brought to bear on the text: looking at genre, language and content, before personal affective interaction and considered response is developed.

Poems were once described by the critic Frank Kermode as 'concerned with intuited truth, not with what is discursively explicable by the reason,' (Kermode, 1957:128). The imaginative space which poetry allows the reader is exactly in the realm of 'intuited truth', and that is what gives the reader the widest range of intuitive possibilities—while and after reading.

It is, however, true that the very density of poetry, its syntactical fluidity and its allusiveness, can create difficulty even for the most expert reader. So, in language teaching, poetic texts are the most problematic in terms of selection, accessibility and usefulness. Modern poetic texts are not necessarily more accessible than older texts, as is usually the case with prose. T. S. Eliot, Dylan Thomas, Philip Larkin, Marianne Moore, Sylvia Plath, and Amy Clampitt all present considerable problems for the reader unused to reading poetry. Hence, most probably, many teachers' wariness of poetic texts.

Single poems can, however, say 'what oft was thought! But ne'er so well expressed'—as Pope memorably put it. Some accessible examples are to be found in textbooks listed in the bibliography: from 'Ben Battle was a soldier bold' to 'a, rose, thou art sick', and from 'I wandered lonely as a cloud' to 'They fuck you up, your Mum and Dad', they represent aspects of human experience in direct but intuitive, concise but rich terms.

Some readers will never get very 'into' poetry, just as some of the more humanistically inclined among us find difficulty in connecting with any kind of scientific or mathematical discourse. The final example is a very good indication of how a poem can be simple and direct, yet with resonances, difficulties (largely only lexical, however), and deep concerns which make it a strikingly usable text with language learners even at an intermediate level. As a pre-reading stimulus, students might be asked *(a)* to identify who is speaking, and/or *(b)* to pick out lines and images they find particularly striking.

Prayer Before Birth

I am not yet born; O hear me.
Let not the bloodsucking bat or the rat or the stoat or the
        club-footed ghoul come near me.

I am not yet born, console me.
I fear that the human race may with tall walls wall me, with
        strong drugs dope me, with wise lies lure me, on black
        racks rack me, in blood-baths roll me.

I am not yet born; provide me
With water to dandle me, grass to grow for me, trees to talk
        to me, sky to sing to me, birds and a white light in the
        back of my mind to guide me.

I am not yet born; forgive me

For the sins that in me the world shall commit, my words
    when they speak me, my thoughts when they think me,
    my treason engendered by traitors beyond me, my life
    when they murder by means of my hands, my death when
    they live me.

I am not yet born; rehearse me
In the parts I must play and the cues I must take when old
    men lecture me, bureaucrats hector me, mountains frown
    at me, lovers laugh at me, the white waves call me to folly
    and the desert calls me to doom and the beggar refuses my
    gift and my children curse me.

I am not yet born; O hear me,
Let not the man who is beast or who thinks he is God come
    near me.

I am not yet born; O fill me
With strength against those who would freeze my humanity,
    would dragoon me into a lethal automaton, would make
    me a cog in a machine, a thing with one face, a thing, and
    against all those who would dissipate my entirety, would
    blow me like thistledown hither and thither or hither and
    thither like water held in the hands would spill me.

Let them not make me a stone and let them not spill me.
Otherwise kill me.

This poem is one of the most successfully stimulating representational texts I have used—at almost any level of language teaching. Not only does it give a narrative 'I' who does not exist, but it touches upon issues of life and death which all students can recognise. What they do recognise encourages them to make the effort with what they don't ('the club-footed ghoul', 'water to dandle me'). The discussion can range from childhood to adulthood, from dictatorship to freedom; and on to the pros and cons of abortion, if class and teacher so wish.

Such rich texts are not easily found, but a teacher with an avid reading curiosity will be constantly on the look-out for usable and stimulating texts. I have learned from dozens of teachers about texts they have found stimulating, and feel that an information pool of such texts would be an ideal resource: collections of materials could be built up, stored and consulted—but that might not be possible in this world. Although, to quote Tennyson's 'Ulysses',

'Tis not too late to seek a newer world.

Prose

The following text is clearly about two characters. A traditional approach might concentrate on who they are, or what happens in the passage. But a pre-reading question which concentrates on the *reader* will give a more useful starting-point for language learners to get something out of the text.

> *At first reading, which of the* two *characters do you sympathise with more, Virginia or Mrs Bodoin?*

So poor Virginia was worn out. She was thin as a rail. Her nerves were frayed to bits. And she could never forget her beastly work. She would come home at tea-time speechless and done for. Her mother, tortured by the sight of her, longed to say: 'Has anything gone wrong, Virginia? Have you had anything particularly trying at the office today?' But she learned to hold her tongue, and say nothing. The question would be the last straw to Virginia's poor overwrought nerves, and there would be a little scene which, despite Mrs Bodoin's calm and

forbearance, offended the elder woman to the quick. She had
learned, by bitter experience, to leave her child alone, as one
would leave a frail tube of vitriol alone. But, of course, she
could not keep her *mind* off Virginia. That was impossible. And
poor Virginia, under the strain of work and the strain of her
mother's awful ceaseless mind, was at the very end of her
strength and resources.

Mrs Bodoin had always disliked the fact of Virginia's doing a
job. But now she hated it. She hated the whole government
office with violent and virulent hate. Not only was it undignified
for Virginia to be tied up there, but it was turning her, Mrs
Bodoin's daughter, into a thin, nagging, fearsome old maid.
Could anything be more utterly English and humiliating to a
well-born Irishwoman?

Most students will sympathise with Virginia. It is to be hoped
that one or two might sympathise with Mrs Bodoin (although it
has to be admitted that neither is actually particularly sympathetic!). What is more interesting is to ask *why*.

The word 'poor', applied to Virginia, almost automatically
encourages the reader to sympathise with Virginia; and by the time
the word has been used three times in the first paragraph, it has
acquired resonances which go some way beyond the unreferenced
denotational meaning it necessarily had in the first line. The reader
understands why she is 'poor Virginia'; therefore 'poor' now
contains, implies, indeed *means* all the reasons why she is described
as such.

The passage seems at first to be more about Virginia than about
her mother—we learn more about the one than the other—with
completely new information about Mrs Bodoin, which might well
alter or add to our understanding of her, kept back until the very
last words.

It is useful to encourage students to pick out 'key words'; here, in the second paragraph, most would choose 'hate(d)'. A strong word like this, repeated in various forms no fewer than three times in two lines, is easily identified as a key word. It is not advisable to have rigid ideas about what might be a key word unless it is as obvious as this. Otherwise, a key word can simply be a word which a reader latches on to as significant for his or her interpretation of the text. As such, the choice is of course valid, but is more of a personal reading than is the case here.

'Hate' tells the reader more about Mrs Bodoin; and the adjectives she chooses—in lines which students can themselves locate if asked to find Mrs Bodoin's opinion of her daughter ('thin, nagging, fearsome old maid')—would tend to influence the reader towards sympathy for Virginia, if he or she was undecided.

This can show, if only in a slight and subjective way, how an author (in this case, D. H. Lawrence) can play with readers' emotions and reactions for his own ends. Does he want the reader to sympathise more with Virginia? It seems so, from this reading. Students might now begin to wonder why he should want to do so; however, hypothesising about what the author wanted to achieve, say or mean is beset with traps for the unwary.

Better to explore areas which can offer clearer interaction with the text:

- **prediction** (as in, 'What do you think might happen now?')
- **discussion** (as in, 'Do you think Virginia was right to go out to work?')
- **evaluation** of character ('Think of some adjectives you would use to describe Mrs Bodoin.')
- **imaginative extension** ('How do you think Virginia feels about her mother?' 'What title can you give to the text?' Here, there should be a multiplicity of answers, which will confirm the open nature of the text. Any of

the titles given will reflect an attitude to the text, a possible interpretation. It is worth underlining this straightaway, as one of the most stimulating and appealing features of a representational text.)

In every case, students should be encouraged to refer as much as possible to the text to back up their answers.

More technical questions can lead more deeply into textual detail; they move a little more into the area of stylistics, but that need not put teachers off if they want to go on with the same text. The usefulness of any text depends on how much students and teachers enjoy continuing to work with it. When it stops being useful, stop; and sum up what has been achieved, in order to consolidate in students' minds the learning payoff the text has given.

More technical questions might focus, for example, on:

- **graphology**: the differences between the two paragraphs both in terms of 'look' and content; the italicised 'mind' in line 13 – Who gives it the emphasis?
- **phonology**: Are there any memorable sound patterns, or alliteration? (the crescendo of *v*- and *f*- sounds in the second paragraph, for instance);
- **vocabulary**: Does any of the vocabulary impede comprehension? What about the imagery—'thin as a rail', 'like a frail tube of vitriol'—does it help create a picture? Can students think of similar expressions in their own languages? (or better ones?);
- **syntax**: Is there anything unusual? (Perhaps the emphatic inversion in line 19, 'Not only was it ...', and the repetition later in the same sentence, 'her, Mrs Bodoin's daughter', which stress Mrs Bodoin's strength of feeling.)

Any of these can be brought out, but they should be brought out *from* the students, rather than explained *to* them. A little guidance may be needed to help them see what will then seem obvious —but that is precisely what teaching reading is all about.

If the first text was focused largely on character, the next looks at first sight like a simple dialogue (and the graphological 'look' of a reading text is always psychologically important, even subliminally, in its effect on the potential reader). As students read, however, it may become more than just any conversation. The pre-reading question is designed to open up some of the text's possibilities.

As you read the text for the first time, try to decide (a) how many characters there are, and (b) what their precise relationship is to each other.

One day, when he sat talking with his 'uncle', he looked straight into the eyes of the sick man, and said:

'But I shouldn't like to live and die here in Rawsley.'

'No – well – you needn't,' said the sick man.

'Do you think Cousin Matilda likes it?'

'I should think so.'

'I don't call it much of a life,' said the youth. 'How much older is she than me, Uncle?'

The sick man looked at the young soldier.

'A good bit,' he said.

'Over thirty?' said Hadrian.

'Well, not so much. She's thirty-two.'

Hadrian considered a while.

'She doesn't look it,' he said.

Again the sick father looked at him.

'Do you think she'd like to leave here?' said Hadrian.

'Nay, I don't know,' replied the father, restive.

Hadrian sat still, having his own thoughts. Then in a small, quiet voice, as if he were speaking from inside himself, he said:

'I'd marry her if you wanted me to.'

The sick man raised his eyes suddenly and stared. He stared for a long time. The youth looked inscrutably out of the window.

'*You!*' said the sick man, mocking, with some contempt.

Hadrian turned and met his eyes. The two men had an inexplicable understanding.

'If you wasn't against it,' said Hadrian.

'Nay,' said the father, turning aside, 'I don't think I'm against it. I've never thought of it. But – but Emmie's the youngest.'

He had flushed and looked suddenly more alive. Secretly he loved the boy.

'You might ask her,' said Hadrian.

The elder man considered.

'Hadn't you better ask her yourself?' he said.

'She'd take more notice of you,' said Hadrian.

They were both silent. Then Emmie came in.

The passage is immensely useful in making students aware of questions of cohesion. 'He' in line 1 is later referred to in several ways—'the youth' (line 7), 'the young soldier' (line 9), and 'Hadrian' (from line 11). Similarly, 'the sick man' (lines 2 and 4) is called 'the sick father' (line 15), 'the father' (line 17), and finally 'the elder man' (line 35). These are the only two *active participants* in the dialogue.

Emmie comes in at the very last line (it is interesting that her arrival does not merit a new paragraph). So she is not really an active participant in the action but, with Cousin Matilda, she is a *passive participant*. There are, therefore, four characters in the passage, although only two are active participants.

The mentions of 'uncle' and cousin seem to imply a family relationship; perhaps the old man is father of the two girls, Matilda and Emmie. This still leaves us a little in doubt over Hadrian's precise position. Here the graphological effect of the single inverted commas at 'uncle' (line 1) is of fundamental importance, telling us that the older man is' not a real uncle, but is called 'uncle' by Hadrian. That is all we can deduce—but the deliberate ambiguity of these relationships is part of what makes the passage open. (Hadrian is, in fact, adopted, but this is not revealed in the passage, so it is important to deduce something about the relationship from the graphological evidence.)

Comparing this text with the one about Virginia, the passage is almost completely in dialogue form, and hence the layout on the page is very different from the dense two-paragraph layout (one long, one short) of the first passage. The pace of the conversation is slow: this can be confirmed by the repetition of words to do with looking ('stared', for example) and with stillness, with reflection and considering, all of which suggest a slow rhythm of movement. Emmie's entry in the last line is perhaps intended to break this air of slowness and silence, creating tension maybe as to what might happen next. Silence is important throughout, contrasting with the spoken words. There are no obvious key words, but the ideas of looking and of silence are repeated, thus taking on some importance. Again it is difficult to pin down what the passage is *about*, although it is clear what happens in it. Perhaps the reader's sympathy is not drawn on; the reader merely watches the situation developing. No message then—just a description?

Of course, the individual reader will note different things and react differently, catching a clear message where another reader finds only description. What is important is to see the range of possible elements to explore.

Questions and tasks can be set to look for: semantic elements which confirm the pace of the dialogue; the most significant words (in each reader's opinion); the locality (Rawsley, an unknown place —would the text have been different if it had been Manchester or Edinburgh?); Hadrian's job, motivations and ambitions (a lot of scope here); dialect forms ('Nay', 'If you wasn't against it'); the feelings of Emmie and/or Matilda; prediction; the complicity between the older and the younger man; male attitudes/female passivity; provincial life/escape; and so on.

Contrasts within a text are always useful for exploitation: between the beginning and the end (what has happened?); between characters (any number, active and passive); between paragraphs; even between sentences. These contrasts take the reader beyond basic 'wh-' questions very quickly, and open up areas of conflict, of *narrative tension*, which are intrinsic to the imaginative appeal of any representational reading text. Contrasts can almost always be found in a text and will almost invariably give the reader enough material for discussion of the themes of the passage, as well as the possibility of giving concrete references from the text to back up analytical and interpretative affirmations.

If we move on now to a text that seems at first to be more a description, we will find more contrasts which can usefully lead to a wider discussion of a range of themes and ideas..

As you read the text for the first time, pick out the main character. Then decide how the last paragraph is different from the rest of the passage.

But under all this, things were not well. The very next morning came the farm-boy to say that a cow had fallen over the cliff. The Master went to look. He peered over the not very high declivity, and saw her lying dead on a green ledge under a bit of late-flowering broom. A beautiful, expensive creature, already looking swollen. But what a fool, to fall so unnecessarily!

It was a question of getting several men to haul her up the bank, and then of skinning and burying her. No one would eat the meat. How repulsive it all was!

This was symbolic of the island. As sure as the spirits rose in the human breast, with a movement of joy, an invisible hand struck malevolently out of the silence. There must not be any joy, nor even any quiet peace. A man broke a leg, another was crippled with rheumatic fever. The pigs had some strange disease. A storm drove the yacht on a rock. The mason hated the butler, and refused to let his daughter serve at the house.

Out of the very air came a stony, heavy malevolence. The island itself seemed malicious. It would go on being hurtful and evil for weeks at a time. Then suddenly again one morning it would be fair, lovely as a morning in Paradise, everything beautiful and flowing. And everybody would begin to feel a great relief, and a hope for happiness.

Then as soon as the Master was opened out in spirit like an open flower, some ugly blow would fall. Somebody would send him an anonymous note, accusing some other person on the island. Somebody else would come hinting things against one of his servants.

'Some folks think they've got an easy job out here, with all the pickings they make!' the mason's daughter screamed at the suave butler, in the Master's hearing. He pretended not to hear.

'My man says this island is surely one of the lean kine of Egypt, it would swallow a sight of money, and you'd never get anything back out of it,' confided the farm-hand's wife to one of the Master's visitors.

The people were not contented. They were not islanders.

'We feel we're not doing right by the children,' said those who had children. 'We feel we're not doing right by ourselves,' said those who had no children. And the various families fairly came to hate one another.

Yet the island was so lovely. When there was a scent of honeysuckle and the moon brightly flickering down on the sea, then even the grumblers felt a strange nostalgia for it. It set you yearning, with a wild yearning; perhaps for the past, to be far back in the mysterious past of the island, when the blood had a different throb. Strange floods of passion came over you, strange violent lusts and imaginations of cruelty. The blood and the passion and the lust which the island had known. Uncanny dreams, half-dreams, half-evoked yearnings.

This is clearly a more advanced text than the previous two. But the pre-reading question is designed to focus attention on a specific part of the text rather than on the whole passage. The global sense of positive/negative events in constant contrast can be grasped even at a first reading.

What emerges as possible subject matter for discussion here can cover: man and nature; the spirit of place; the Master and the island; past and present; selfishness; money. Any of these themes could be developed by going into the text as superficially or as deeply as the single class or teacher decides. A fairly superficial reading will bring out contrasts between good and bad, positive and negative, inhabitants and island and this can easily suffice as exploitation of the text. Specific items ('the lean kine of Egypt' as a biblical reference, for instance) need not necessarily be gone into, since the passage is clear without their having to be handled.

By way of illustration of what the passage might give students if the teacher is prepared to take a rather more 'stylistic' approach, we can look at the first and last paragraphs and construct a fairly detailed analysis.

The contrast between the beginning and the end of the passage is usually significant. Here, the first paragraph and the last paragraph can very usefully be compared and contrasted. This is a possibility frequently offered by longer passages of several paragraphs.

The turning-point of the whole passage is the single contrastive connector, 'Yet' (line 36). It introduces a completely positive paragraph about the island, but differently from the rest of the passage, there is no mention of any people on the island. The island here begins to live, breathe, smell, have a past, have a life. The colours become more alive; blood red is the dominant colour. Several words are repeated ('yearning', 'longing') and their effect on the reader is subtly conditioned by the personal pronoun 'you' (lines 38 and 41). Who is this 'you'? It is, of course, a general 'you', but it has the effect of drawing the reader personally and directly into the narrative, of involving the reader with the living, breathing, true nature of the island. There is a direction of sympathy here, because the reader comes to sympathise with the island and, by implication, to lose sympathy with the people, who do not seem to appreciate the positive aspects of the island—they want money out of it (there are references at line 5 to 'expensive' and at line 27 to 'pickings'). A vital contrast, then, is that between appreciation of the island and lack of appreciation of it.

Syntactically, it is worth noting that as this sympathy is being built up almost impressionistically—through light, colours and smells—in the last paragraph, the author begins to dispense with verbs. The direct narration of facts and events has given way to an evocation of the island, which began with 'so lovely': the reinforcement contained in 'so' was already an appeal to the reader's emotions.

If we now look closely at the first paragraph of the passage, we will be able to see (a) how it contrasts with the final paragraph, thus confirming the reading of the text as being more about the island than the people on it, and (b) how it is possible to say something about almost every word. (Exhaustiveness is not to be encouraged, however! Students would not appreciate having to plough their way through a mass of detail about a whole text; but *close reading* of vital sections of a text can be very useful in backing up an interpretation.)

'But', the very first word, indicates a contradiction of what has gone before (which the reader cannot know), confirming the pattern of alternation between positive and negative we have already noted. 'This' is an exophoric cohesive reference to what has been described, presumably positively, as can be seen from 'things were not well'. 'Under' implies two levels of appearance, the surface and the deeper level: this can perhaps be linked to the surface life of the people on the island and its contrast in the last paragraph with the deeper life of the island itself.

The second sentence contains a syntactical inversion of subject and verb—which perhaps adds to the effect of rapid change contained in the word 'very'. The word is, in fact, not strictly necessary to the meaning of the sentence, but it gives reinforcement to that meaning. Any such literally 'unnecessary' word is worth commenting on, since it creates a deliberate stylistic effect, as here. There is a small contrast in the use of the articles in the second part of the sentence: 'a cow' suggests there are many, while 'the cliff' would seem to refer exophorically to a geographical feature already known to the reader. This is also the first reference to imply the nearness of the sea: the island itself is not mentioned until line 10. It is this sentence which contains the only *plot* element of the paragraph, with the fall of the cow.

The next sentence introduces the principal human character in the passage, and graphologically his position and importance are stressed by the use of the capital letter: he has no name in the whole text, nor do any of the other characters. They are given professions or roles rather than personal identities. This perhaps confirms the contrast between the long-term identity of the island, as communicated in the final paragraph, and the lack of identity of the people temporarily living on the island.

The verb 'look' is followed by words indicating timidity or lack of conviction in the Master: 'peered' is a weak word, and 'not very high declivity' reinforces the negative implication. The sentence, much longer and more flowing than the others in this paragraph, moves from a stress on weakness (with reference to the Master) to a stress on colours ('green', and the bright yellow of 'broom')

which gives prominence to Nature and the naturalness of the
island.

The final two sentences of the paragraph are in free direct
speech, with no main verbs—the omission of the verb will recur in
the final sentences of the last paragraph. The free direct speech
here takes the reader into the Master's mind and contrasts beauty
with waste, stressing the importance of money in the adjective
'expensive'. The final word, 'unnecessarily', and the graphological
effect of the exclamation mark which follows it, show the Master's
judgement of the cow and its fall. The word 'unnecessarily' means
it is a problem the Master could do without, but it also implies his
lack of understanding of Nature and of natural events, which is the
root problem of the whole passage.

Few teachers will want to go so painstakingly through one paragraph in this way, but *analysis* of this kind is the furthest step in the
use of representational materials without its becoming Literature
study. As such, it takes students more deeply into the mechanisms
of a text, helps them to justify their interpretations and, in particular cases, builds an immensely useful bridge between the use of
representational materials and the stylistic study of literary texts.

9 APPARATUS AND TECHNIQUES

Abilities and functions

WHAT IS LEARNED AND WHAT IS TAUGHT IN SECOND language reading? If reading is a process of decoding a written message, there have to be several levels of decoding/receiving/understanding involved. It is very rare with imaginative reading materials that any reader, even reading in his or her mother tongue, achieves 100% understanding of the written text, especially when reading for pleasure rather than for study purposes.

Reading involves some knowledge of the language being read and of its system of writing. To this basic enabling ability, the reader of imaginative written materials must bring some or all of the following:

- reading curiosity or interest;
- ability to recognise what is written, and interact with it;
- deductive, intuitive, and interpretative abilities;
- some world knowledge with which to relate to the author/text;
- some shared knowledge with author/text;
- motivation.

Reading representational materials goes beyond simply the extraction of information, and therefore beyond the usual requirements of 'reading comprehension' or those of the apparatus which normally accompanies a language-learning reading text.

Imaginative materials—or, roughly, literature—can have several functions, explicit or otherwise:

- a factual function (information)
- a sharing function (reassurance)
- a challenging function (subversion)
- a descriptive function (evocation)
- an explanatory function (didacticism)
- an assertive function (propaganda)
- an escapist function (entertainment)

and any one (or more) of these, together with sundry hidden functions on the more emotional level: making the reader laugh or cry; surprising, thrilling, frightening the reader; and so on.

So reading comprehension, as such, hardly scratches the surface of what a representational text can do, *by*, *with*, and *through* the language it uses. Consequently, many features of the standard question apparatus—most significantly, multiple choice questions about the basic meaning of the passage—begin to lose their usefulness. Neither is the development of skimming or scanning techniques, or of summarising or memory skills, of paramount importance in the first instance; although, naturally, all of these elements will have a place in the overall programme of developing interactive reading skills.

The tasks or activities set will not only determine what students get out of the reading but also how they go about it. An overview of the sense of the text will emerge in answer to a good overall pre-reading question, and the text can be *skimmed* in order to provide the answer. *Scanning* is closer to information search, as the reader finds specific answers to specific questions or justifies assertions of opinions, and so on.

With representational materials, students are encouraged to expand their reading competence in various ways:

* extension of reading range

This covers not only variants in lexical and syntactical choice, but also the length, style and content of texts read. It goes hand in hand with:

* extension of reading scope

Reading representational materials involves much more than information search or comprehension, as we have seen. It involves reading for pleasure. The appreciation of word-play and textual openness, the capacity to cope with various points of view, considerations of humour and irony, imagery and figurative language all have to be considered. This implies also:

* extension of affective reading

Emotional and intellectual involvement is inevitable in representational reading. Students may or may not be well-equipped as effective affective readers in their own language. Helping them to become so in an L2 context can therefore sometimes involve a return to the basics of subjective reaction, in terms as simple as liking and disliking. From such acorns, considerable oaks of reading enjoyment can grow.

Stages in teaching

Exercises, worksheets, and tasks come in a multitude of shapes and sizes. A quick glance at any books containing representational materials (see the bibliography) will show that there can be no cut-and-dried way of exploiting the texts.

However, certain areas must be covered in an apparatus. These might include:

- pre-reading presentation ('warm-up');
- pre-reading stimulus/question (and follow-up);
- vocabulary;
- comprehension;
- extension.

These could be shown in diagram form:

```
                        Pre-reading
                             ↓
                         Stimulus
                             ↓
                           TEXT
                             ↓
              Post-reading: Immediate reaction
         Specific tasks: problem-solving and enabling activities
           Problem areas: vocabulary/comprehension, etc.

                        Development
                      ↙            ↘
            Subjective                Objective
               ↓                         ↓
           Response                 Clarification
                                   (of mechanisms, etc.)
                      ↖            ↗
```

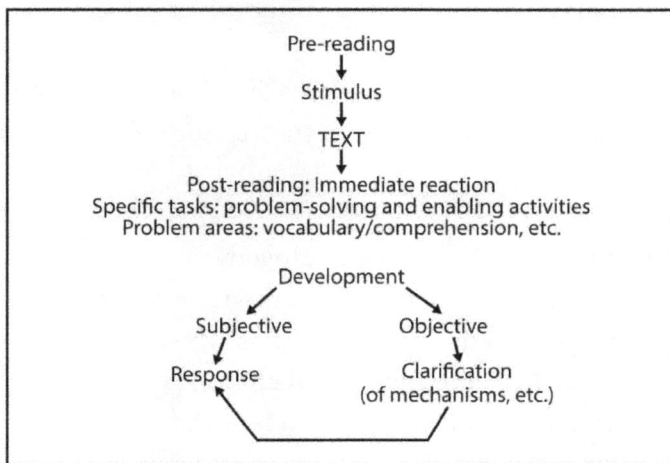

The balance between subjective and objective depends on teaching aims. It is obviously neither necessary nor desirable to understand every unfamiliar word, for example. Teachers and students do, however, enjoy vocabulary work if it is presented in some of the more active ways (rather than by simple anticipation): mix and match, multiple choice, clustering, rewriting (implies syntax as well as lexis), guessing within semantic areas, deduction, modernising (of archaic forms), standardising (of dialect or other variant forms).

This done, many teachers feel that the greatest part of their work is over because the greatest impediment to 'comprehension' has been coped with; a true/false exercise can check up on any doubtful moments, and some 'wh-' questions will clarify the facts of the matter. This is reductive in the extreme, applicable perhaps to referential materials, but hardly in a representational context. For these are all *low order* tasks or questions. Representational texts invite the reader to move on fairly rapidly to *high order* questions, probing the interpretative possibilities of the text, and beginning to look at the author's presumed intention, at the connotations and implications of what is written, at the wider subject matter the text touches upon.

The extreme of the objective approach will lead to close textual analysis, and to an understanding of such features of the text as

- lexis (words)
- syntax (how the words are put together)
- cohesion (the linking mechanisms within the text)
- phonology (sounds)
- graphology (the look, and visual effects)
- semantics (areas of meaning and how the meaning is achieved)
- dialect (usually spoken variants on standard English)
- register (tone)
- period (archaisms, fusions of genre, etc.)
- function ('message', 'author's intention', etc.)

This will in turn permit the reader to comment on the *style*, which is the beginning of stylistic analysis, and is not part of our concern here.

The subjective side of the picture takes us into the areas of opinion, discussion, evaluation, acceptance, and rejection. Critical judgment, of content perhaps rather than of style or form, becomes a part of the process.

Transformation of context and register as part of an apparatus can be a mixed blessing:

You are a reporter on the Verona Gazette. *Write an interview with Lord Capulet after the deaths of Romeo and Juliet about the problems he and his family have gone through.*

This kind of exercise is, I feel, wrong-headed and counterproductive. It implies that *Romeo and Juliet* is a series of facts that might be found in a newspaper, a chronicle of disasters that befell the star-cross'd lovers. Almost, indeed, a referential text. It also implies a needless attempt to update and reformulate, ignoring the original work's own terms of reference, function, and impact. There is no need for responses to be superficial, naive, or reductive.

Teaching techniques with representational materials go beyond reading skills; they bring in speaking and writing practice in discussion, debate, and extension (written work), as well as encouraging extensive reading. They involve reinforcement techniques through occasional summary work, recall of previous reading, and the encouragement of cross-reference to an ever-growing range of texts.

Perhaps listening should not be ignored either; since the teacher will very often read the text aloud or play an audio recording, students are encouraged to develop an ear for sound, sense, tone, register, humour, effect, and quality.

As the novelist Bernice Rubens once put it: 'The acid test of a good piece of writing, even if it is of violence and cruelty, is that it must make one's ears water. One cannot *teach* the music of words, but one can teach its awareness, and out of that awareness it is possible that the ear will learn offence, and take to tuning itself.'

'Awareness' is the key word here: awareness not only of language as a means of conveying information, but as enjoyable in itself, for the effects it creates and the results it achieves. It is useless to ask such questions as, 'How does the text become charged with meaning?' Most language students (and, I imagine, most literature students) would not have the first idea as to how to answer that question. It is an example of a teacher, or materials writer, imposing his or her presuppositions on the learner: the critical viewpoint here is given more importance than the original content.

Towards interaction

Representational texts do not reveal reality in the way that referential texts do. Theirs is a mock reality; at a slight (or great) remove from what is known as reality. This reality gap must be bridgeable if the author is to succeed in communicating his message. Most textbooks, methodological approaches, and, I fear, teachers, still tell students what to think. The communication gap is not to be bridged in that way. It is mono-directional, apart from anything else, whereas the teacher's role should be as an intermediary between author, text and receiver—opening up a multi-directional sphere of interaction.

An apparatus, therefore, must be an enabling device or series of devices, rather than a test or a selection process. The apparatus has to open up the text, rather than close or limit it. To some questions ('wh-' questions, for instance) there will be right or wrong, true or false answers. But, as the move away from lower order questions takes place, the emphasis will be more and more on affective questions, which open up the text rather than insisting on correctness.

Discipline is needed, therefore, on the teacher's part in order to avoid students going into flights of fancy and departing too much from the text. Questions have to be properly focused to take the reader *on* from whatever answer emerges. Wrongly focused questions will tend to have no particular usefulness beyond the giving or finding of the answer. (Yes/no questions or, worse, questions which invite or create mystification, can stultify interest and demotivate the students considerably.) The best questions are open; they are, in the best sense of the term, *leading* questions.

'Justify your answer with close reference to the text' will become a stand-by during discussion of representational materials. This becomes vital in terms of learning pay-off, and in helping students to realise what has been learned through the reading and discussion.

Identification ('wh-'?) can occasionally cause difficulty, especially in time shifts. For example, this sentence from Walter Scott's *Ivanhoe* presents a very obvious and frequently found area of difficulty for L2 readers:

> This proclamation having been made, the heralds withdrew
> to their stations.

'Having been made' is the syntactical heart of the problem. Reformulation, by students, might result in, 'The heralds withdrew to their stations after the proclamation had been made.' (We do not know, out of context, if the heralds themselves made the proclamation.) Questions such as, 'Which came first: the proclamation, or the heralds' withdrawing?' are helpful in clarifying the syntactical problem of time identification; but the fundamental point is that the effort expended is not really worth the result gained. The text as it stands gives the reader no imaginative stimulus: it can be used as a simple rewriting exercise, but its usefulness ends there.

Teachers have to judge what students can get out of a text, even out of a single line. If the only benefit is technical (as with the line from *Ivanhoe*), it is better not to bother. It is wrong to use a text purely because it contains a 'problem' of this kind which the teacher wants to illustrate (or 'teach'). Intrinsic interest must take precedence over discrete item input; the grammar of literary texts is not what we are teaching.

Pre-presentation

An imaginative text should never be introduced 'cold'; that is, without some kind of preliminary preparation. This can be as simple as a 'warm-up' exercise, an introduction to the subject matter, or a recap of something already done. It is best to tailor the introductory activity to the kind of text you are going to work with, rather than fall back on clichés like, 'Today we're going to talk about...' or (worse), 'Today we're going to read about...' What the text is about will, to a certain extent, be a question of interpretation, and the danger of closing some of the potential avenues of interpretation is always inherent in any introductory mention of the text being 'about' something.

The most important single thing to bear in mind is the relevance of the text being used to the students and to the course they are following. If the text is carefully chosen, the problems of presentation are thereby greatly alleviated. When the text is taken from a course-book, the teacher should be helped by the teacher's book in finding a suitable variety of ways to present the text. When the text is independently chosen, by the teacher or a colleague, the reasons for choosing it should clarify the reasons for the students reading it.

This pre-presentation or introduction phase is largely to do with reasons for reading the text, such that students can appreciate why the text is being read and can be motivated towards a useful reading of it.

The presentation phase can be of several kinds: *linked, initiating,* and *search* are the most common.

A *linked* presentation will emphasise how the present text relates to work previously done. The relationship may be purely linguistic ('Remember last time we talked about what would happen if ...? Today we're going to look at something similar'). This may call for some recap language practice, by way of reinforcing the work done previously and preparing for the text to be read. The link is more likely to be conceptual or thematic, however. We saw in Chapter 6 how the thematic approach can bring together the most diverse kinds of text. Very often the link is then of this type: 'We're going to look at another approach to.../view of.../treatment of...' Again, a recap—however brief—of work already done, or a reference to texts previously read, is useful in focusing students' attention on the subject matter and in giving them a point of comparison to which they can refer.

An *initiating* presentation is used the first time a subject is introduced. So the pre-presentation may take a little longer, as ideas are exchanged, brainstormed, suggested by the teacher, offered by the students, etc.

A *search* presentation is the 'coldest', but in some ways the most involving way of introducing a text. It involves students tackling the text immediately, with a view to finding out one or more things from the text. This is only advisable when (*a*) the text contains a number of easily found items (of any kind, linguistic or thematic), and (*b*) the text does not present any particular reading problems. Group and pair-work motivation in the search reading can be increased by a kind of competition, if the search stimulation is of the 'How many ___ can you find?' variety.

It should not be necessary—and can indeed be demotivating for the reader—for the teacher to anticipate the content of the text to be read, to give a kind of pre-reading summary. It is a temptation that we can all too easily fall into in our keenness for the students to understand the text, but it is quite probably motivated in us by our own uncertainty as to whether or not they will understand it. The teacher's own confidence in the materials to be used is vital: hence the importance of careful text selection, stressed earlier.

The pre-reading stimulus or instruction is the single most important part of the apparatus accompanying any text. It confirms whatever brief presentation or linking introduction the teacher may want to give and, most usefully from the student's point of view, gives a precise indication of what the reader is to do with the text.

The formula 'As you read...' is probably the easiest way to give the instruction. It is, however, important to show rather than to anticipate: 'As you read, you will find...' is not to be recommended, for example. On the other hand, 'As you read, try to find.../look for.../pick out...' makes the reader *do* something constructive. This can be as simple as picking out key or theme words; listing the characters; evaluating the participants in the action in basic terms (positive or negative, sympathetic or unsympathetic); deciding on authorial or narratorial tone of voice (only when it is obvious and a main feature of the text); or even just deciding what the passage is 'about'.

This pre-reading stimulus (or focus) gives students a task to do, *which must be within their capabilities,* regardless of the complexities the text presents. This can easily be taken to absurd lengths (finding 'a' sounds in a passage from *Finnegans Wake,* for example); but the students' achievement of some or all of the task set can then be capitalised on, in order to go more deeply into the text.

It should be borne in mind that it is neither necessary nor even desirable to go into every text to the same depth and extent: some texts are better touched upon and left after two or three readings; others will reward much more close reading. Teachers here have more liberty than materials writers, who normally have to furnish as complete an apparatus as possible for every text; but an apparatus is there to help, so teachers and students can make as much or as little use of the apparatus as the particular teaching/learning situation dictates.

Post-reading

How and when students proceed to the post-reading apparatus will obviously depend on how many times the text is to be read, and how carefully. Ideally, there should be no reason for students not being able to respond in some way to the pre-reading stimulus after the first reading. Their ability so to respond is more important than the total accuracy of their responses at this stage: as more meaning emerges from the text on further readings, initial intuitive and almost wholly subjective reactions will become more considered, more informed, and more aware, and so will become rather more objective responses.

The phases or stages of a single lesson can be identified as:

- pre-presentation
- interaction and developing response
- pre-reading stimulus
- first reading
- further reading(s)
- follow-up and reactions
- exploitation
- second reading (specific tasks)
- further work

These phases correspond, very roughly, to the language-teaching sequence of 'presentation—practice—reinforcement'. It is not really advisable to try to make out a lesson plan in this context, as one might do for a language lesson. (And the lesson or lessons should not be considered as a 'teaching unit'—the term is not applicable in this context.) Instead, these phases can be indicated together with some other necessary considerations, so that the headings might be:

- level
- learning objectives/curriculum
- time allowed/individual lesson objectives
- phases and techniques

Communication about the text, reaction, and response to the text should be the foremost objectives in the teacher's mind. So any presentation, linking the text thematically, say, to texts previously read or discussed, must be kept brief, and should arouse learners' interest in what they are about to read. It must not get in the way of the text's communication with the reader, but should facilitate and encourage that communication. In the present context, author, title and the period of the text do not concern us, and are not a necessary part of the pre-presentation. They can be examined and discussed later, as further work, if desired.

At the first reading, the students should both read and hear the text at the same time. The exercise is neither reading comprehension nor listening comprehension, but exposure to the full passage, with a view to reacting and being able to give an answer to the pre-reading stimulus.

The text may be read by the teacher. Problems of pronunciation, teacher inhibition, and so on should not get in the way: confidence is all, and the teacher does, after all, know the passage quite well, having prepared the lesson(s) on it! Alternatively, a recording (or even a video) may be used. It is important at first reading to go through the text without stopping. Pauses, re-hearings, and repetition can wait until the second or subsequent readings, when students have an idea of the text as a whole.

Follow-up simply picks up on the pre-reading stimulus for immediate answers, reactions, and impressions. These will clearly be subjective, but are intended only to verify that the reading has given the students something to latch on to, to catch their interest, and to use as a jumping-off point for all the rest of the work to be done.

Rapid comprehension checks can be made here—using 'who' questions, characters' names, and so on—simply to fix the text a little more in students' minds before going on to specific tasks to be carried out during the second reading. This stage is brief, but vital; if the second reading follows immediately from the first, without this space to gather first impressions and subjective reactions, these valuable interactive insights will be lost. They should be the basis for much of the subsequent language work and discussion.

The initial post-reading tasks or questions should take up from the pre-reading stimulus, going more deeply into the aspect of the text foregrounded there. This might mean focusing on vocabulary, if there is a particular density of unknown words, although these earliest tasks should concentrate on helping the student get something valid out of the text despite vocabulary problems.

The specific tasks assigned for during and after the second reading will probably focus on problem areas: vocabulary, syntax, contrasts, special effects, key words and ideas, etc. The order in which subsequent tasks or questions are arranged is flexible and will depend on what is to be got out of the texts and the problems the texts present. So, once again, the learning objectives—the reasons for reading—have to be clear.

With a literary passage, there is a great risk of treating the text too superficially. If anything, this is worse than analysing it in exhaustive detail. The teacher must guard against these two extremes. Once the teacher has established the priorities for a text, the students can go on, confident that their reading and work on, in, and around the text are justified, and will lead to a clear goal.

What to avoid

Questions such as, 'What effect is the author trying to achieve here?' or 'Do you notice that the sentence starts with a rush and then slows up? How is this achieved, and what is the effect?' will generally be treated with total bafflement in an L2 context. The second involves the questioner standing in front of the text, to point out what he or she considers an important feature, rather than leading the reader to the discovery of the effect. 'Why should Keats have chosen to use this mediaeval form?' (in 'La Belle Dame Sans Merci') will only be answered by 'I don't know.'

An apparatus is not just a series of questions. It is almost useless to present a text and simply follow it with questions, no matter how well thought out the questions may be. Students must be introduced to a text and given an indication of what they can get out of it before they start reading. The habit of reading and listening at the same time also fundamentally influences the type of apparatus a text will have.

Questions should not lead to answers like 'Yes' or 'No' unless they lead to or from some significant point. Questions which produce the answer 'I don't know' are to be avoided at all costs. This may seem too obvious to need stating, but it is a trap that teachers and materials writers can easily fall into. The point to be brought out might be clear to the teacher and not to the student; hence the breakdown in communication.

What the apparatus should do is help the process of negotiation between student and text. It should be a process of clarification and revelation. Too much terminology or teacher talking (exposition or, more brutally, standing in front of the text) will only lead to demotivation and obfuscation.

There can be several useful headings to parts of the apparatus: Vocabulary, Comprehension, Imagery, Comment, for example. But if these are to be used, they should not be found with monstrous regularity, following each and every text in mechanical fashion. How the post-textual apparatus is organised will depend on the problems the text raises and the uses to be made of it; it will depend on the pre-reading stimulus and instructions, and on the single text's relationship to the other texts it is grouped with, if any.

It is also vital for native-speaker teachers and materials writers to get out from under the shadow of British 'Eng lit' study techniques. Literary awareness, and the habit of reading, cannot be assumed. The resulting risk of being patronising and overly didactic has to be guarded against at all times.

Only at the highest level of tertiary study are most L2 students able to cope with the complexities of close textual analysis. At most levels, comprehension is the fundamental problem. The first requisite of the apparatus must therefore be to show students *what* is to be comprehended and to indicate *how* it can be comprehended. To this extent, the apparatus is necessarily guilty of guiding first responses, and thus the first stages of interpretation. There is no reason to object strongly to this, as long as it is counterbalanced later on in the apparatus with an opening-up of interpretative possibilities and the opportunity to reconsider opinions and interpretations, through comparing and contrasting with other texts.

It is essential to start on fairly secure ground. Once students have acquired a sense of security and a certain freedom in moving about—both within a single text and working with two or more texts—then the less secure ground of open interpretation can be explored. This building of student confidence is the first, and arguably the most important, function of the apparatus. It should, especially in the early stages, introduce concepts or approaches that would otherwise be likely to come between the student and the text, and thus hinder interaction.

The apparatus, together with the experience of reading and listening to the text, should create the possibility of ever-increasing interaction. Once that has been established, further critical approaches, challenges, interpretations and hypotheses can begin to be played with, in the confidence that something firm has already been got from the text.

Tasks and questions

It is useful to make a distinction between tasks and questions for several reasons. Questions imply answers, and educational habits tell us that answers are usually right or wrong. A task, often a 'finding' exercise or a comparison or evaluation exercise, when used with representational materials, will show that we are not necessarily working in the realm of clear-cut answers; the expressing and justifying of opinion is what we are aiming at, rather than selection of correct items, or simple decision-making.

This is not, of course, to throw question-and-answer techniques in all their variety out of the classroom window. But questions should stimulate research into the words of the text, decisions about meaning possibilities, deductive and intuitive understanding of what has been read. A question whose usefulness is over as soon as the answer is given is, more often than not, an unproductive question. Good questions lead beyond their answers.

Multiple-choice questions and true/false questions are, in this sense, mechanical and limited. They are useful for checking comprehension, and for bringing out lexical choice differences, but should be seen as a fairly rapid *enabling* exercise rather than as the be-all and end-all, as they frequently are in reading comprehension.

It is best, therefore, to build up a linked series of questions which serve to help the reader through the text, to unravel the knots which may impede understanding, and to piece together the overall communicative intentions of the writer, as far as they can be gauged. The answers, which will involve degrees of 'correctness' varying from straight right or wrong answers to completely open interpretation, will thereby serve to help the student towards an individual reading of the text, without imposing a reading on it.

Of course, as we have already seen, any text selection and apparatus necessarily reflects the teacher's or the materials writer's view of the text, and it can easily happen that an apparatus restricts the interpretative possibilities of a student's reading. The teacher should be on guard against this; and should also beware of criticising someone else's textual apparatus because it does not reflect his or her own ideas!

There is no ideal balance of tasks and questions, just as there is no such thing as an ideal apparatus. What seems a lot to one teacher can seem too little to another. No teacher or class is forced to follow an apparatus slavishly, however, and careful lesson preparation (with the help of a teacher's book or notes in the case of published materials) will show the teacher how much or how little will need to be done with the class for whom he or she has chosen a particular text.

Vocabulary

Vocabulary is one of the most vexed questions in the teaching of reading and the use of reading materials. It is fairly commonly asserted that, say, ten new words in a passage of one hundred words make the passage problematic for the student. The teacher's solution should not be to reject the passage just because of lexical difficulties, but to find ways of diminishing the problem *in terms of students' receptiveness*. I have been at pains to stress the importance of reading and listening together, and of clearly delineated pre-reading tasks with deliberately restricted aims, in order to help students to the psychological satisfaction of reading the text to the end. At that point, students' receptiveness has overcome a great deal of the inherent resistance to unfamiliar lexis, and vocabulary exploration can begin from the positive achievement of something already understood.

This is why, in general, I am not in favour of vocabulary anticipation before the early readings of a text. However, there may be occasions when a key word or expression, if not glossed beforehand, will cause confusion, and discourage students while they are reading. The anticipation of more than a very, very few words is usually counterproductive, and may reflect the teacher's lack of confidence in the materials he or she is handling.

A running glossary (in the margin or in footnotes) can be useful in passages for extended reading, i.e. of more than about two pages in length. In this context, vocabulary acquisition takes second place to reading achievement, and the glossary should be designed to help the reader along, without constant guessing or dictionary work.

In a glossary, or in some cases of vocabulary anticipation, direct translation can save a lot of useless effort. To gloss 'sheep', for instance, as a 'wild or domesticated... timid, gregarious, woolly, often horned, ruminant of genus *avis*' is rather less than helpful to an L2 student! The judicious use of translation of single words or, occasionally, idiomatic usages will not interfere unduly with the essential objective of thinking in English through contact with representational materials.

It would be ostrich-like, however, not to recognise that in many countries representational materials in English language teaching are still handled by a great many teachers of the 'read and translate' school. An awareness that translating is a quite separate and distinct skill, involving a range of techniques which are quite different from language teaching and learning requirements, must be ever-present in the mind of a teacher using any kind of reading materials in the language classroom. Translation, in this context, is not even an easy way out, as the student makes no effort to think or interpret in the target language, derives no interest or stimulus from the context of the text, and is left struggling with the ramifications of representational language without ever knowing why he or she is reading any particular text, or deriving any L2 learning benefit from it.

Several kinds of lexical tasks can be exploited: straight dictionary search is possible, and dictionary-using skills should be developed. But instead of leaving students to plough their way through the text, looking up words they don't know (or think they don't know), dictionary activity should be structured, and task-based. This can be done in various ways: matching up words with their meanings in context; filling in grids or charts, where logic or education gives the answer; choosing the most apposite from a range of synonyms or alternatives; word-building (i.e. arriving at the word from a suggested cognate).

Most textbooks nowadays use such a range of techniques; variety, and the encouraging of a sense of discovery, are of the essence here. The same kind of exercise with every text leads to demotivation and boredom in the student. And since vocabulary use, playing with words, exploring their resonances and effects, is fundamental to the enjoyment of imaginative writing, vocabulary work on representational materials should be backed up with vocabulary evaluation: 'Which word is more effective, the original or the synonym?' or, 'What difference does one word make to the overall meaning, impact or effect of the phrase or sentence?' These questions, and variants on them, serve to bring out the difference between, to quote the example used in Chapter 5, *grimy* and *dirty* to underline the value of lexical variants, to give an awareness of how writers can play with words, and consequently how readers can play with their meanings and effects.

Of course, students may get the wrong end of the stick and overdo the playing aspect of lexical discovery. Enrichment of passive vocabulary does not mean that the newly discovered words can be used *ad lib* in active production. It is vital, therefore, to stress the use of lexical items *in context*—only by an acquired familiarity with a range of contexts will students be able to play correctly with more obscure or 'literary' words.

Nation and Coady (in Carter and McCarthy, eds., 1988:108, 110) show how syntactic clues are more useful in helping students guess unknown words than discourse level clues. In fact, discourse analysis, though immensely useful for teachers in the present context, is slightly beyond the reach of most language learners. Teachers can, and should, learn from studies in discourse, but should beware of thrusting them intrusively into language-learning courses.

Nation and Coady usefully suggest (page 110) this five-point strategy for guessing unknown words in texts:

(a) find the part of speech of the word;
(b) examine the immediate context;
(c) examine the wider context;
(d) guess the meaning;
(e) check that the meaning is correct.

I would stress the importance of semantics at point (b). The text can give clues as to the semantic field of the unknown word, and students can decide whether or not to proceed further with that word. It is important that students realise that they can stop at any point on this scale when they are satisfied with their knowledge both in relation to the reading and for their own reasons.

A mention should be made here of *core, non-core,* and *subject-core* vocabulary.

Core vocabulary is the basic vocabulary which is central to the lexicon (*dirty* but not *grimy*, for instance).

Thin is core. *Skinny, slender,* and *lean* are non-core, and show values or judgments, qualities, or degrees of thinness, in relation to the core word.

Subject-core vocabulary means vocabulary which is specific to a subject, such as scientific discourse, where terminology is restricted in its use and application. (See Carter and McCarthy (eds.), 1988:171-176 and Carter, 1987:33-45 for an excellent brief summary of the question.)

What this involves in relation to representational materials is the question of *lexical choice*. Representational materials usually give non-core vocabulary, in that the author is deliberately moving away from the most basic concepts towards a richer, more subtle expression of the ideas he or she is handling. I would not go so far as to assert that referential materials use core vocabulary and representational ones use non-core, but a predominance of non-core lexical items has to be seen as one of the more positive aspects of working with representational materials.

Clustering exercises can help students appreciate levels of lexical choice. From the core word *dirty*, the cluster can be built up:

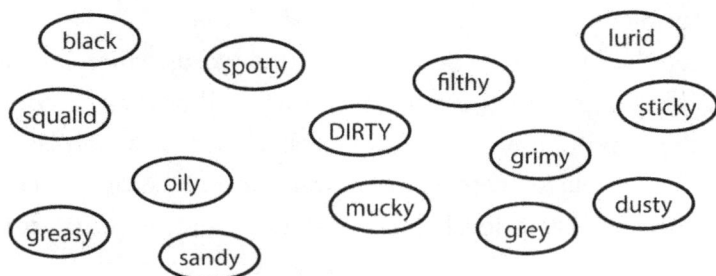

Of course, the sequence *dirty-filthy-lurid* implies a scale of values and a range of application which L2 learners have to become familiar with. One would rarely describe the cooker as 'lurid' after making Sunday lunch, but a story in the Sunday newspapers could be—and both could be filthy!

This is lexical choice at its most practical and rewarding for students. They can be encouraged to build up vocabulary clusters on all kinds of core words: *tree* leads to *forest, oak, leaf,* and *branch*, for example. *Move* leads to all kinds of verbs of movement, with speed, means of transport, etc., implied. Adjectives are especially valuable in terms of 'quality' and point of view; adverbs, for levels of character and reaction.

Clarke and Nation (1980) (quoted by Carter, in Carter and McCarthy (eds.), 1987:178) ask the following questions, which deserve reflection. 'Does the skill [of guessing words from context] transfer from one language to another? Will practice in guessing in the mother tongue automatically result in improvement in guessing in the foreign language, and vice versa? Is a score on a cloze test a reliable measure of how well a learner can guess word meanings? How much does practice with cloze tests develop the skill of guessing word meanings?'

I have considerable reservations about the use of cloze procedures on representational texts with L2 students, despite encouraging work done on the subject—and interesting use made of it in, for example, Carter and Long's *The Web of Words*.

There is, I feel, little point in omitting words which learners are unlikely to know in the hope that they will suggest a core word and, thereupon, appreciate the lexical choice of a non-core word when it is revealed. This is, I am aware, to reduce cloze techniques to a culpably basic level; but what can be done with advanced students, who already have a degree of literary awareness and training, is not necessarily applicable to language learners with no such skills.

There has to be a clear distinction made between *enabling* activities and more literary *exploring* activities with representational materials: vocabulary clustering work is a more readily accessible way of examining the same area of study, while cloze work may make demotivating demands on the less literary-oriented learner. (However, see Carter, in Carter and McCarthy, eds., 1988:161-80, and Carter, 1987:177 -81, and the bibliographical references he suggests, to balance out this point of view.)

Syntax

Many of the observations on vocabulary hold good for syntax too. It has to be said that, although English grammar is a vast subject, the basic range of structures and tenses is actually fairly small, and not unduly inaccessible to the willing L2 reader, who might be quite unable to produce the structures he or she can passively comprehend. The syntax of prose, and of modern narrative prose in particular (apart from 'stream of consciousness' narration), should not normally present great inherent problems to the L2 reader if the texts are carefully chosen and apparatused. Poetic diction presents a range of different problems.

The unravelling of syntactical knots often has to be handled through *reformulation*. Milton's

> *and, had the earth been then, all earth*
> *Had to her centre shook*

can be reformulated to read

> *and all earth, if earth had existed then, would have shaken to her*
> *centre.*

Clearly, texts which present this kind of problem are more likely to be used with more advanced or specialist students. However, the fundamental point is relevant to all levels: the apparatus must help the students with the key task of *identification*. This can be necessary even at the apparently obvious level of identifying subject, verb, object, and such things as cohesive elements and relative pronouns. Endless confusion can be caused through students' failure to identify these elements correctly in a text.

Again, the solution is not necessarily to reject the text, but to ensure that the apparatus helps the students over the problems which are likely to arise. A series of simple questions regarding reference ('Who does "he" refer to?') and identification can rapidly clear up these potential confusion-makers, and can also help to train students to recognise English techniques, especially in cohesion.

On occasion, the pre-reading stimulus will contain an element of identification anticipation, perhaps naming character(s), or giving a preliminary clarification of potential problems of identification, cohesion and connectors. These can help smooth out what otherwise might become syntactical difficulties, and the listening-while-reading process should smooth over some other potential difficulties of a similar nature.

If new or relatively unfamiliar grammatical points are to be encountered in a reading passage, the teacher should decide on the usefulness of dedicating time to that point in a different lesson, such that the reading consolidates the grammatical input. Some frequently-found stylistic or syntactical features, such as emphatic inversion ('only when... did I...', 'not only did he...', 'so bad was it that...', for example) hardly need comment in the overall context of the passages in which they are separately found, but are worthy of remark, and of special concentration if applied to students' own written work.

As with lexical variants, syntactical variants should be evalu-ated by the students, their effects considered, especially in compar-ison with 'expected' forms or with what the students might themselves have written. The question, 'How would you have phrased this?' can lead fruitfully to this kind of evaluation of both *what* has been said and *how* it has been said.

A logical development from this can be the discovery of elements of patterning, repetition and rhetorical devices in a text. It will not be necessary for non-specialists to give names to most such devices; recognition that an effect has been gained through language is, for the L2 reader, more intrinsically important that examining it in detail.

The kind of eliciting question used in any discussion of stylistic effect should steer clear of suggesting the answer. This kind of question stands between the text and the reader; for instance: 'See if you can comment on the *elegance* of the writing.' The same inten-tion would be reached better with, 'What adjectives would you use to describe this kind of writing?'—perhaps also giving a few adjec-tives to choose from ('formal', 'stately', 'elegant', 'colloquial', 'sloppy', or something else), such that the choice has to be thought about, the various possibilities weighed up, discussed, evaluated. 'Justify your opinion' will then become a common feature of the apparatus, if the readers are considering an open series of possible choices, reactions and interpretations.

Towards discussion

Exploitation may imply discussion, debate, writing (at home or in class), research (into the subject matter, the writer, or whatever)— production based on what has been read. *Further work* continues this but, importantly, can lead to the reading of the whole text (especially in the case of a short story) from which the passage studied has been extrapolated. Comparative reference to other texts can be made at either the exploitation or the further work stage. This will bring the teacher back to the important preliminary question of how the particular text relates to others in an overall curriculum.

In this way, the apparatus should always be working towards the interactive possibilities that the closer reading of the text opens up. These, it is clear, are not only thematic, although the theme will be both the inspiration for and the keynote of most of the spoken and written production stimulated by the text. Discussion should be encouraged about the text itself: its language, its expression, its tone, its style, as well as its content and its thematic links with other texts. Thus, students begin comparing theme-linked texts in terms that go beyond the theme but are, in fact, derived from it; the theme link is the peg on which a range of discussion possibilities can hang.

It is vital to avoid unconnected activities in the apparatus. A variety of activities is to be encouraged, but a clear aim should be kept in view, and each activity should in some way help the student

towards that goal—be it comprehension, interpretation, evaluation, or merely aware reaction and response.

We also have to bear in mind the amount of class time available
for reading, for working through the apparatus, and for discussion.
It is often necessary, in order to allow for discussion time, that
some of the apparatus be given as homework; it can later be
consolidated in written production and a useful, two-phase homework pattern encouraged.

Discussion—in pairs, in groups, or in the form of debates or
whole class interaction (teacher-controlled)—should be a prime
feature of work with representational materials. Not all the
possible avenues of discussion can be explored with every text.
Usually, several points have to be left by the wayside since the
texts, if well-selected and well-exploited, will prove rich in discussion stimuli of various kinds.

Similarly, it will usually be unwise, particularly in a non-
specialist context, to try to examine or analyse every possible
feature of a text: there is such a thing as doing a text to death. We
will do well to bear in mind A. E. Housman's words, in the context
of just how much meaning (or anything else) we can get out of a
text we are studying:

> Even when poetry has a meaning, as it usually has, it may be
> inadvisable to draw it out. ... Perfect understanding will
> sometimes almost extinguish pleasure.

One result of this wide range of discussion possibilities is what
might be called the 'time-bomb effect'. Naturally enough, the texts
should provoke thought, reflection and response in the readers.
Not all of these reflections will emerge immediately: there are, in
many cases, both short-term reactions and responses, and longer-
term responses and re-evaluations. These should be cultivated, as
they reflect not only the possibility of comparison with later read-

ing, but the constant use of what has been read as a point of reference. It develops reading memory, memory reference search and recall—and begins to build up in the students' minds that reading frame of reference which will become a useful part of their cultural baggage.

Something might be said here about *verification*. During every stage of work on the passage, the teacher will keep an ear open to make sure that the passage is being understood; although, as we have said repeatedly, reading comprehension as such is not what interests us here. 'Verification', in this context, is preferred to 'evaluation' as a term to describe a test or examination situation. Clearly, the teacher should not be primarily interested in whether the students have read and remembered the passages they have worked on. What should be considered is how they talk or write about what they have read, how well they refer to the texts, how much of a frame of reference they can use in comparing and contrasting the various texts they have studied. This is a true verification of reading competence, and a bringing together of language and reading skills.

The place of appreciation

'Appreciation' is something of a bugbear. Courses are taught on it, books are written about it and, sadly, it has become something of a drudge, something to be got through, something that has very little to do with *le plaisir du texte* (to quote Barthes) or reading enjoyment.

Critical appreciation involves the working out of what a passage says, and possibly also how it is said. It is part of the progress towards writing a commentary or a critical essay; something that is very much part of the British L1 educational system in secondary schools and at tertiary level. It requires an ability that most L2 students never acquire, even in their own language. As such, despite its academic credentials, 'critical appreciation' is not really part of the communicative interaction with representational materials in an L2 context.

Specialist students may very well have to be able to write an essay or a commentary on a single text. The best way to learn this particular skill is through comparing and contrasting several texts, until an appreciation of what a text is doing, and how and why, is acquired. Again, however, this is a specialist skill in literature study.

Reading and listening

It cannot be overstressed how important it is that students listen to and read extended passages of representational material at the same time. The text (or texts, in a theme-based programme, for example) comes to life when read or performed; it comes off the page, and becomes very much more than either simply a reading text or a listening exercise. (See 'Accessibility', Chapter 6.)

Many coursebooks containing representational materials (stories, scenes, theme-linked texts) are now published with audio recordings available, and these can be an invaluable resource. This is not only because of the immediacy they can give to the reader's encounter with the text, but also because the performed version offers an *interpretation* of the text which the readers can interact with, accept or reject, discuss and evaluate. A vital extra dimension is thus given to the material, while accessibility is facilitated and enjoyment potential enhanced. Students often ask to be permitted to copy the cassettes, for their own rather than class use. This is usually not allowed by copyright, although it happens all the time. Publishers will, I feel, have to come round to the idea of lower-priced students' cassettes for representational materials.

Of course, cassettes are only available with published materials. But no teacher should ever feel inhibited about 'performing' a representational text, or about reading it aloud with no deliberate performance element. Every time a teacher stands in front of a class, there is some element of performance; the more the teacher enjoys it, within the limits of the aims of the lesson, the more the class will enjoy it too. In this way, literature can come to life, and regular listening while reading will become a part of the methodology of using representational materials.

Jigsaw reading

This technique, whereby students, singly or in groups, read separate sections of a text and then exchange information on it—usually through question-and-answer or oral summary—in order to build up the complete picture, is widely used in referential language work. It is applicable to representational materials also, but with the proviso that its usefulness lies largely in the seeking out and communicating of information—and a representational text is usually doing more than just communicating information.

Like any single technique, it can be used *when appropriate to the text*. It is useful with longer texts and in extensive reading (students reading alternate or selected chapters of a full-length novel, for instance). It is a useful language-practice exercise with reading materials, precisely because of the language production it entails, and the student-centredness of the activities it stimulates.

Judiciously used, jigsaw reading can be a useful regular technique with representational materials.

Reading aloud

The practice of having students read texts in English around the class is largely counterproductive. It imposes constraints of pronunciation, concatenation, and understanding on texts which are better used for interactive purposes.

There are many better ways of practising or testing pronunciation and concatenation. The exercise of reading aloud is so artificial that, even if students do understand the text completely, any achievement in learning terms is, in itself, rather superficial. Few of our learners are going to use this skill unless they become foreign-language newsreaders!

Using drama materials for pronunciation, as well as for their representational content, is immensely productive and enjoyable for both teachers and students. Some distinction has to be made between using drama for what might be termed 'theatre workshop' purposes, and using dramatic texts as representational materials for language learning, where the dramatic activity becomes an extra factor in class use of texts. This specific area is examined in depth in my *Using Drama in the Classroom* (see bibliography), but the principles for the use of representational materials hold good whether the texts used are prose, poetry or drama.

Games, role-play, etc.

Enough has been written about games, role-play, and so on, for the aware teacher to evaluate their usefulness in any language-teaching situation. They can equally well be used with representational materials—but only if teaching aims are clearly kept in focus.

The imaginative engagement in ludic learning is often an attempt to reach students and involve them precisely at the levels of curiosity, fantasy, interaction, and self-expression that representational materials encourage. So the only word of caution I would sound is that the activity must always lead students somewhere: there must be a learning payoff. And it is important that this payoff not be too distanced from the text used; nor should the text just be an excuse for a ludic activity. All activities must contribute to the interaction of student and text, or develop from that interaction towards a recognisable goal, an appropriate learning achievement.

An activity, however enjoyable, that is only an end in itself will not give this kind of learning satisfaction.

Archaism

Old forms of English are sometimes adduced as creating difficulty for L2 readers. But, in fact, most of the simpler forms of archaic language can be handled fairly easily when first encountered. *Thee/thou/thy* as second person *you* have equivalents still in use in several languages. A text like William Blake's 'The Fly' is simple and effective enough for this particular language 'obstacle' to be assimilated easily, if students are given a pre-question which focuses on the specific item, while leading on to the theme of the text:

As you read, underline the pronouns which show differences between 'I' and 'thee'.

> *Little Fly,*
> *Thy summers play,*
> *My thoughtless hand*
> *Has brush'd away.*
>
> *Am I not*
> *A fly like thee?*
> *Or art not thou*
> *A man like me?*
>
> *For I dance*
> *And drink & sing:*
> *Till some blind hand*
> *Shall brush my wing.*
>
> *If thought is life*

And strength & breath:
And the want
Of thought is death;

Then am I
A happy fly,
If I live,
Or if I die.

A follow-up question should immediately lead to identification of the participants—the poet/speaker/narrator and the fly/addressee—without the archaisms causing too much hesitation. The text can now be opened up for discussion, reformulation (rewriting, experimenting with different verse forms, for instance), and evaluation.

Often it will be helpful to have students rewrite archaic language in a more modern form: in this case, using *you* and *your*, for example, to reinforce the newly learned forms. It should be clear that a few such items (*hath* for *has*, *wert* for *were*, and so on) can be easily handled. However, too dense a quantity of archaism will make a text less accessible and might weigh against its use in class, especially at lower levels of language learning.

Recognition of archaic forms is, however, an important part of language awareness. It should be related, if possible, to the history and development of students' own language: students often have little familiarity with the history of their language and, in my experience, find it a fascinating subject to examine.

Archaism is one of the most common variants from standard present-day usage in *any* language, so attempts to avoid using it in a language-learning situation are misguided. There is no need to 'protect' students from encountering what is, after all, a perfectly natural phenomenon. An awareness that language is in a constant state of flux is essential to a proper understanding of how language works, how it is used, and what it achieves.

The word 'brush'd' in this text gives students an opportunity to examine *lexical expansion*. They may recognise 'brush' as a noun, and may even have come across it as a verb, in the context of hair, clothes, etc. Here 'brush'd away' means 'killed'. The fairly ordinary word has been expanded, carrying the implied action well beyond its normal application, and coming very close to metaphor in the way it is used.

Students need not go much beyond recognition in how they cope with this kind of lexical expansion. But recognition will be vital in demonstrating how words can expand and contract their meanings and frames of reference—how words play and can be played with. (The word *brush* could be further explored in such contexts as *brush off*; two people brushing against each other; a brush with the law; brush up your idioms, and so on; whereby students are invited to describe the meaning of each use in their own words, but without consulting a dictionary.)

Other Englishes

A similar and very closely related question to that of archaic language is that of so-called 'new' Englishes, starting with American English. Students are culturally aware of America and Britain as separate forces, and the Coca-Colanisation of the universe has led also to an awareness that American English sounds different from other Englishes, and has some orthographical and lexical variants also.

These variants cover spelling (*honour/honor*, *plough/plow*, etc.) and occasional common words (*autumn/fall*), but do not in fact create real problems of accessibility in written texts. Cultural and geographical references may very well be more impenetrable in American English than purely linguistic features.

Local Englishes (Indian, Caribbean, African) are becoming more and more expressive in their own ways, rather than imitative of British or American English. Most writing freezes examples of language use. With the passage of time, these writings gradually become less accessible; the language changes, assimilating new influences almost daily.

The texts used in most EL T textbooks are written in fairly standardised British or American English and, sadly, the examples of representational language usually offered to L2 readers reflect this. But every regional or continental variant produces a rich, expressive range of representational materials. Learners will at first prefer to acquire a familiarity with something more accessible than dialect or archaic texts; but, again, reading while listening will help the student over the initial hurdles of these variants. (I use the word 'variant' in preference to 'deviant' throughout, in view of the rather negative connotations of the latter; as well as wishing to avoid the implication of some 'norm' which is being 'deviated' from, especially in this context.)

Students in countries where English is a second language will naturally find different sets of problems. Some references may be familiar because they have been assimilated into daily use in L1, while the grammatical system has to be learned from scratch. Bengali is a case in point, since a fair amount of vocabulary ('table', 'post office', etc.) has come into the language from colonial times: basic referential communication is actually helped in a way by this. In this particular case, some verb forms (to have a cup of tea, to have a meal) also aid L2 familiarity. But this process stops dead at the referential level in a very high number of learners.

The mother tongue in class

This is a vexed question which should not create vexation at all. The amount of L1 or L2 used in any classroom situation depends on a wide range of factors:

- student motivation;
- topic interest and accessibility;
- students' linguistic ability
- active/passive thresholds;
- teacher encouragement;
- practice and habit.

Most teachers of English world-wide are not native speakers of English. And it has to be recognised that a great many non-native speakers are very much better qualified and more highly motivated than some native speakers who drift into English language teaching. There is no need whatever for non-native-speaking teachers to feel in any way that they are second-class citizens of the ELT world. Indeed, many of us can benefit—and have benefited enormously—from working closely with teachers whose first language is not English.

Very elementary students will naturally have a limited range of vocabulary and structures with which to react and respond in English to representational materials. What is important is that the teacher gauge the desired reaction and response, and not try to go too far. Translation of students' reactions can help them find confidence in their opinions and their ability to express them, and they will gradually be able to build up an interactive capacity from the basic, limited area of:

'What do you think?'
'I don't like it.' / 'I like it.'

Some representational materials now contain specific enabling sections, to encourage students to find their feet in English in the context of such materials.

The texts are in English; the teacher should use as much English as possible; and the students should be encouraged to formulate their reactions, responses and any extension work in English. Thus an atmosphere is created which is conducive to thinking in English, enjoying the language encountered, the content and the interactive processes that result.

The occasional word translated, or the expression of opinion in the students' own language, is a perfectly natural phenomenon. It should be used as a link to English, rather than as an impediment to—or an avoidance of—the use of the target language.

The more students can learn not to seek direct equivalents in lexical terms between their own and the target language, the more they will be able to appreciate lexical choice, to evaluate what they are reading, and to liberate themselves from the dictionary and the denotational trap. The flight from equivalence is a vital part of representational learning and learner development.

10 EVALUATION

THE QUESTION OF THE EVALUATION OF STUDENTS' progress as readers of literature, or, at a less ambitious level, the assessment of the progress made within the course or curriculum prescribed, has been touched upon briefly (Chapter 9), but cannot just be left to a postscript. A whole new field of assessment procedures is opening up. Testing procedures in language teaching have been experimented with and refined considerably in recent years. Objectivity is one of the key elements in most of those procedures: to verify whether or not the student has achieved a certain level of capability and/or fluency in the target language.

Jonathan Culler—several years ago now—gave one of the best rationales of examinations; it still holds good in our present context, even though it was originally applied to literature study— albeit with a small 'l' (see Chapter 6). A general sense of 'how to read' is what we are after, although Culler takes his point further, towards a 'common base of reading... to make explicit the conventions which make literature possible' (in Schiff (ed.), 1977:66). This final aim is not part of language teaching as such, but indicates the beginning of the grey area, when reading representational materials begins to encroach upon the study of literature.

If we are to get away from Culler's 'read and remembered' examining of literature study—in other words, if we are not simply testing students' reading memory—we are faced with the difficulty of deciding precisely what *is* being tested. It is almost inevitable that some element of subjectivity will enter into the examining process, but a few constants can be established which will begin to delineate the scope of examinations in learning with representational materials.

Almost of necessity, there is what might be called the language part of the examination. Whether it be a written or an oral examination, the students' ability to use the target language accurately and fluently will always be a vital component, if not the major component, in an L2 learning context. Representational materials may very well be used simply as a means to that end, as a valuable element in language practice and in the development of various skills. Indeed, the purpose of this book has been to encourage such use of representational language.

If the learning objective is only linguistic, then there need be no worry over testing procedures, as long as the student is given the chance to talk and/or write about something with which he or she is familiar. This may mean talking about texts, writers, contexts or themes; it may mean offering options and comparing points of view. The representational materials used are, therefore, the springboard for the language production being tested; what is tested, however, is as much as possible the *language production*, rather than, for example, the critical evaluation of what has been read, or the acceptability of the learner's opinions.

It is when the use of representational materials implies a wider range of learning objectives that new guidelines for evaluation techniques are required. What is to be avoided at all costs is the syndrome of 'competitive sensitivity' or 'informed sensibility'.

Sensitivity and sensibility are enormously dangerous words in this context, implying some kind of aesthetic elitism in the appreciation of literature and other arts that is both wrong-headed and pernicious. They imply, in a rather Leavisite way, that the student who is most sensitive to an author or a text, or who is most receptive to an imaginative work, will be the best able to discuss it or to give a good examination answer on it. And if this sensibility or sensitivity is combined with an ability to use acquired information on period, author, philosophical background, metrical techniques, and what have you, so much the better for the final examination result.

This approach implies a pantheon, a 'great tradition' whereby Milton is unmistakeably greater than Clough and, consequently, more worthy of the students' attentions. No matter how important a part of our cultural background such a 'great tradition' may be, and no matter how significant an awareness of this critical outlook is in our time, it has to be stressed that concepts of English studies are changing. Milton will remain 'greater' than Clough, but not simply because the major critics tell us so; rather because Milton's texts themselves give us more to investigate, to discuss, to evaluate, and to refer to our own situations as well as to their original contexts. But Clough's texts are interesting, stimulating, and valuable: 'major' and 'minor' are classifications that tend to limit rather than expand the reader's horizons.

It may very well emerge from extended study of texts by the two writers that the reader does in fact subscribe to the received critical evaluation of Milton's relative worth as against Clough's. But we are not actually in business to run a kind of Authors' Top Twenty. Even those who teach 'Eng Lit' and were brought up with the 'great tradition' will find many writers to whom they themselves would deny a place in the panoply despite their establishment therein by tradition. Personal taste, i.e. the subjective element, comes in at every level of this kind of discussion, and there is no easy or convenient way to suppress it. On the contrary, some element of personal reaction and response to representational texts is, as I have maintained throughout, indispensable. How, then, can this necessary subjectivity be reconciled with the objective requirements of language testing, without falling into the 'sensibility and sensitivity' trap?

One essential element must be comparison: the learner's capacity to compare and contrast texts will show not only the linguistic capabilities and level reached, but will apply that linguistic achievement to a personal evaluation of the content, theme, style, context, and effectiveness of two or more texts. The expanding frame of reading reference, discussed earlier, is in fact the main basis for the content of the examination or test. This frame of reference can consist of any number of texts, themes, genres, or periods, according to the requirements of the syllabus to be followed.

For the purposes of a literature syllabus, this is infinitely flexible: the range of texts studied can cover one year or centuries, one author or many, one theme or several. The starting point is always the text, however. As it was for teaching purposes, so it must be for testing purposes. Any change of orientation or emphasis between what is taught and what is tested is not only unfair to the students but reflects a dangerous uncertainty and lack of coherence in the teacher's own mind.

The evaluation of student performance in this kind of testing situation will take account of linguistic capabilities (fluency, accuracy, self-correction, etc.):

- the ability to make connections and cross-references;
- the ability to quote and summarise constructively;
- the ability to balance arguments and reach conclusions;
- the ability to take subjective standpoints and relate them to objective criteria;

- the ability to contextualise;

and many others, depending on individual situations. Flexibility is of the essence, and there is no such thing as a perfect answer or an ideal candidate.

In my own experience, oral examinations of this kind are best conducted in groups. As interaction develops between and among arbitrarily grouped candidates, the dangers of the candidate offering a prepared speech are considerably lessened, and all members of the group are required to think and produce, to listen, react and respond, to interrupt, contradict, hold the floor, and justify opinions. Such an examination procedure requires a great deal from a student, but it should be clear that it can function at any level and with any number of texts.

As memory is not being tested, I find no objection to students being able to consult the texts they have read during the examination; indeed, the ability to find apposite quotations to back up an argument is a very valuable one.

The best interactive possibilities in such a test situation will be found with three or (at maximum) four students in a group. The examiner should be slightly outside the group—to prompt, referee, redirect, and occasionally rescue the discussion. If classroom procedures have familiarised students with the interactive possibilities of group discussion regarding representational materials, there need be no undue examination nervousness. Again, the teaching should be closely related to both *what* will be tested and *how* it will be tested.

It may be objected that this system favours the extrovert to the detriment of the quieter, less forthcoming student. This is practically inevitable. It is partly the examiner's responsibility to ensure that each member of a group under examination gets a fair crack of the whip. Any experienced teacher or examiner learns how to recognise the less talkative but no less competent student, and acts accordingly to draw all quieter students into the group or class discussion. Familiarity with the requirements of the test situation should encourage the candidate. There are always those who just do not perform on the occasion; this is a fact of life in the unsatisfactory world of examinations in general.

Marks will be awarded according to the criteria established locally, as dictated by syllabus requirements and so on. It is to be stressed that marks are *awarded,* not subtracted. This is not, like dictation perhaps, a test whereby a perfect standard is set up and all imperfections result in lost marks. The examination or test should give the student the opportunity to show

- what has been learned,
- how that learning has been applied, and
- how that learning can be expressed.

The student who cannot remember the date of birth of the author under discussion should clearly not be castigated. If, however, some awareness of the historical or socio-political background to the text is necessary to the discussion, an inability to make such connections relevantly would imply poor performance, *if the course of reading required such reference.*

A written examination perhaps involves fewer such problems. The decision must be made very early on in the teaching of the course as to what kind of written production is expected of the students, both during the course and in the relevant examinations or continuous assessments.

The only difference between the written production required of students at the end of a course and that done during the course is the extent of the frame of reference encompassed. Some teachers have been known to make the mistake of making a final examination more difficult in terms of content or expectations, or simply in terms of marking standards. Completeness of programme reference is already quite enough to make the examination a valid test of learning achievement. It is totally misguided on the part of the teacher or examiner to apply the kind of double standards which would result in a fair level for classwork performance not being up to the standard of performance required in a final examination. If there are to be examinations, it is a vital part of the teacher's responsibility to make students aware of the level of production that will be required of them.

11 LITERATURE AS A SPECIALIST SUBJECT

Specialisation

THE MAIN DIFFERENCE BETWEEN THE USE OF representational materials as part of language learning, and the use of literature as a specialist discipline for L2 students, is one of *focus*. Where in language learning the emphasis has been on theme or subject matter for the specific aim of language development, in literature study the emphasis will be on text, author, and period. There is no need for the communicative and interactive principles, already found, suddenly to be discarded as we move into the realm of specialisation. English for Academic Purposes need present no more difficulties or arcane mysteries than any other kind of English study.

The methodology so far discussed in this book is wholly applicable to the context of academic English study—say for a degree in English or for a teacher-training qualification. The approaches we have seen are indeed an indispensable introduction to the study of literature. Too often, in university systems all over the world, literature study is not related to language learning; one is considered something of a superior discipline, the other an inferior exercise (often entrusted to lower-level personnel). Language learning and literary study are interdependent and, in a specialist context, should be seen as complementary at all stages in the educational process.

Only in this way can the situation be avoided whereby an L2 learner at beginner or false-beginner level finds that Chaucer is the first author on the programme. The absurdity of learning the different usages of the Simple Present and Present Continuous tenses while battling through the 'Nun's Priest's Tale' may seem far-fetched, but is, in fact, a not uncommon occurrence in English L2 degree courses.

The emphasis on the historical study of literature in an academic context is not threatened by a contrastive approach to selected passages from major and minor writers. The approach is a necessary introduction not only to a wide range of writers, styles and content, but also to ways of looking at texts and of examining them in depth.

Where the exploitation of a text for non-specialist learners may stop short of close examination of, say, metonymy and metaphor, stylistic devices or the historical context of the writing, the teacher of a more specialised class can move on *with the same texts* to investigate those elements that will bring the students into contact with such features of historical language, authorial style and period context that are required in a history of literature curriculum at tertiary level.

The emphasis on the text as the starting-point for all literature study is of paramount importance. The metalanguage of literary study, which can comfortably be avoided in non-specialist use of representational materials, has here to be integrated into the apparatus. Basically, the techniques applied in terms of text selection and grading, apparatus, and classroom practice will remain the same; the variable is the teaching aim. Whether the level is secondary school or university does not actually make a great difference in the initial stages; beginners are beginners whether they are fourteen, twenty, or sixty years old. There is, of course, the question of students being mature enough to handle the themes presented, but, to all intents and purposes, if a group of texts is going to work at all with L2 students, the maturity level and the intellectual level tie in closely with the basic question of accessibility and the importance of what the readers are required to do with the text.

A literature study curriculum has to make greater demands on students. Quite simply, the learning objectives include literary aspects as well as the language-learning aspects which interest the non-specialist teacher and learner. So, in addition to the deeper study of individual texts, there will necessarily be more texts from a wider range of periods and contexts in a specialised programme. The structure of such a programme will move more rapidly to extended reading: from extract to short story to novel, for example; or from a scene to a complete play; or from one poem to a reading of several. The thematic content of one text is thus seen in comparison with an extended thematic and stylistic range. Background, historical context and literary developments, however, are always best related to the text the students start from. To return to an example quoted in Chapter 6, specialist students who have read complementary passages from *Animal Farm* and *Paradise Lost* can refer their reading to the historical, social and political contexts in which these two very different works (which, we have seen, share the theme of rebellion) were written.

I deliberately underline this example in order to show how preconceived notions about author, period or text can come between the student and an interactive reading of the text. Milton, thought of as the creator of an epic poem on the Fall of Man—which was intended to explain Man's 'disobedience' and his place in the great scheme of things—is a considerably more daunting Milton than the one students can alternatively be introduced to, who wrote about the violent rebellion of some independent angels in Heaven. Similarly, the Orwell who is seen writing a sharp allegory against totalitarianism is quite different from the author of a passage where animals take over a farm from humans. The tale, not the teller, must come first—or, as Brecht put it to his actors, 'Show me, don't tell me.' The text is the showing; all the rest is input which comes between the reader and the text. Of course, it is highly relevant and, indeed, useful input. But when information about the text is given *before* the reader has the chance to experience the text for him or herself, it gets in the way; it impedes direct interaction, conditions the reader's reactions and responses, destroys the innocence of reading. Literature teaching has tended to involve too much teacher-talking time, whether in giving background (including names and dates) or in *exposition du texte*. The move nowadays is towards giving more time to reader/text interaction. There is, of course, the grave danger of an overreaction, with the 'facts' (which were all-important to Mr Gradgrind in that model of educational non-methodology described in *Hard Times*) being ignored totally, and reader/text interaction becoming the be-all and end-all. This would be wrong-headed.

In the study of literature, there are many curriculum possibilities. The history of literature remains the most familiar; comparative literature is gaining ground; critical practice is a growing and valuable discipline; linguistics, stylistics and semiotics have shown their worth in the larger discipline of language studies and communication/media studies. This curricular flux is a positive sign: academic disciplines should not be allowed to stagnate and atrophy. English literature programmes in many countries have opened up to the importance of other disciplines, often more rapidly than in English-speaking countries: the work of Saussure, Jakobson, Bakhtin, Barthes, Derrida and others has been widely discussed, evaluated, and incorporated into what used to be a highly insular field.

The step towards interactive reading as a fundamental part of literary education is much less radical, risky or threatening than any of these philosophically-founded innovative approaches. It is a simple practical way of bringing students closer to the texts they read, and of raising their awareness of how to read. There are many valuable books for L1 students which confirm this and expand on it (Traugott and Pratt (1980) is the best), but in the vast world of L2 teaching, very little has actually changed in practical terms of classroom procedure. This is partly, of course, due to traditional gerarchic or hierarchic policies in tertiary education, and to the lower status which many education systems accord to language teaching. It is no part of my intention to tell English lecturers how to teach. What I want to stress is that lecturers in the L2 academic context should complement, encourage and expand upon interactive reading. Courses on interactive reading will lead to students being able to read better, with more awareness and more curiosity, the wider range of full texts which their overall curriculum prescribes.

Ideology

Questions of ideology raise their head in any discussion of the teaching of literature. It is easy for literature to become propaganda, just as it is easy for educationalists—by their choices and exclusions, expositions and silences—to impose culture on the anarchy which they often see it as their mission to avert. In an L2 situation, the pleasure of the text must, however decadently, take precedence over cultural imperialism.

This is not a simplistic avoidance of issues; as teachers, we are not in business to sell 'England's green and pleasant land' or America's grain-filled prairies. There are quite enough cultural, political and economic institutions already busily engaged in doing that. The reading we are directing is an appeal to the individual mind, not a papering-over of class or national divisions, nor an appeal for the approval of either English as the dominant culture or of English literature as the world's richest. It is very interesting to notice that the meteoric rise of English as a discipline is almost contemporaneous with Great Britain's decline as a world power; the Englishness of English shores up the defences against that decline in many theoretical texts on English teaching. But it is the language that is of universal interest and usefulness; cultural use of that language follows closely after. And English, it can well be argued, was secured as a world language by the intervention of the United States of America on the winning side in the First World War.

Gradually, comparative literature is edging its way into academic favour, as the need to defend the Englishness of English literature lessens. We have nothing to fear by introducing non-English literature, or literature in translation, or literature in the learner's language, as part of the representational stimulus to learning curiosity. I would suggest very strongly that any missionary position should be avoided like the plague, leading, as it does, to this kind of assertion:

...we believe that, if rightly presented, poetry will be recognized by the most ardent social reformers as of value, because while it contributes no specific solution of the social problem it endows the mind with power and sanity; because, in a word, it enriches personality.

(From a 1921 report, quoted in Hawkes 1986:114.)

We are not teaching literature as some kind of 'commitment to individualism as a long-term solution to the social problem', an approach which has for so long been the vague but safe guiding light of the study of Humanities. Literature should not be used as a cover-up or an apology: it stands by itself, in each and every single text, as an expression—highly complex and very rarely autotelic or self-delineating—to be received, accepted, rejected, evaluated, discussed, reacted and responded to in a likewise complex manner by the reader who, by accident or external design, happens to come across it. Teacher's choice must encourage learner's choice; the 'canon' of received greatness should, in modern terms, be a self-access bank of texts rather than an institutionalised point of reference. Of course, I too, as most teachers do, have my favourite authors and my pet hates; I acknowledge the 'great tradition', but the mere fact that I express that tradition in inverted commas indicates that it is one way among many of classifying literature as a history of cultural expression.

Innocence and experience

There is almost no such thing as a completely 'innocent' encounter between a reader and a text. Perhaps one or two of the texts we read in childhood have retained that sense of innocent discovery, but to learn (through study or encounters with criticism) that *Alice's Adventures in Wonderland* or the novels of Forrest Reid are not the innocent paeans they seemed is to experience a loss of innocence, to feel a shock of corruption, that all further reading will inevitably compound.

The new trends in literary theory, which have created an unreasonable amount of fear and hysteria in the realms of academe, are no more and no less than the search for a new way of reading literature. It is no longer enough (*pace* Matthew Arnold) to counterbalance culture and anarchy. The movements encompassing structuralism, Marxism, deconstruction, and so on, are working towards a clear and, I feel, valid goal: 'an analysis of the ways in which the meanings of . . . texts have been produced and used: the study of how readings of them arise, operate, conflict and clash, of the social and political positions which they embody and on behalf of which they function.' (Hawkes 1986:123.)

This is literature as a fact of life—there is nothing to be afraid of in looking closely at the facts of life. Reality itself is a plural text, with as many interpretations as there are individuals experiencing it. The text, therefore, is to be considered as an expression of experience: this is the closest we can come to a definition of 'literature'.

Daunting as any '-ism' will appear at first sight, it should be accepted as a means towards exploring the interpretative possibilities of a text rather than as an impediment, forbidding access to the text. Sadly, every '-ism' generates jargon, controversy and factions. Our students, in general, will not have to get involved in the complexities of modes of close analysis of texts, unless they become literature specialists. But teachers who intend to work on texts from a critical viewpoint can benefit from a very basic familiarity with what the new criticism implies; it can be useful, and there is no great mystery or arcane mythology to be unravelled. The literature on Literature, like the literature on language teaching, has grown enormously in recent years. Out of the welter, the books by Wales (1989) and lodge (ed.) (1988) are excellent, accessible introductions to what can be a bewildering area of study. Carter and Long's *Teaching Literature* (1991) is the best recent work on the specialised teaching of literature, and takes proper notice of EFl and the place of literature in language teaching.

The fact that the present book is addressed to teachers working with 12 students does not mean that linguistics, stylistics and so on are out of its scope. The emphasis is simply more on the practical elements of classroom teaching. However, the reader who has borne with me thus far will find that he or she has in fact acquired a familiarity with some of the most basic terms used in linguistic and stylistic analyses of literary texts. I hope some readers will be encouraged to move on to some of the books indicated in the bibliography, although the majority are written, it has to be said, for mother tongue students, often at postgraduate level.

Many UK-based academics working with non-native English teachers have endeavoured, with debatable success, to introduce new techniques in literature study into an L2 context. The main result has actually been to increase the distance between the L2 learner and literary materials, as basic language-learning problems have been given too little consideration. A focus on complete texts, often poems, has also been counterproductive in this context. 'This is too advanced for my students,' continues to be the reaction of even the best-intentioned of teachers when confronted by unrealistic, over-analytical approaches, which tend towards the intellectualisation of the subject.

The 1970s and 1980s produced a welter of new critical schools, from structuralism to deconstruction. These are phenomena of critical fashion, important because they suggest new approaches, new directions, new ways of reading and of thinking about texts. Their importance in the wider scheme of the history of literary criticism remains to be evaluated. We are already in the 'post-structuralist' era but, nothing daunted, the texts live on, unperturbed by readers' and critics' foibles in the way they treat them.

It is reassuring that one of the foremost of modern critics, David Lodge, has one of the characters make the following statement in his 1988 novel, *Nice Work:* 'To be honest, I have had my doubts for some time about the pedagogic application of post-structuralist theory.' He goes on, 'Poststructuralist theory is a very intriguing philosophical game for very clever players.' We do not need to play intriguing philosophical games, either with ourselves or with our students.

The immense value of such critical controversy and debate lies in the very fact that texts are constantly being re-evaluated, re-examined, re-read and rewritten. However, the discussion of critical approaches should never be allowed to drown out the claims made to each individual by the object of all this attention: the text itself.

CONCLUSION

THE POET W. H. AUDEN AFFIRMED IN AN ESSAY ('WORDS and the Word' in Auden, 1968:155): 'The job of the arts is to manifest the personal and the chosen: the study of the impersonal and the necessary is the job of the sciences.'

What we have been talking about throughout this book is that area of human cultural experience which, at one end of the scale, is simple linguistic expression and, at the other, becomes 'the arts'. In no way do I want to assert the supremacy of 'assumptions regarding the value of literate culture to the moral perception of the individual and society,' as Steiner aptly puts it (1967:23). That way madness lies; and an over-insistence on cultural 'values' begs the impossible question, 'are the humanities human?' (Steiner, *ibid.:86.)*

These are tortuous paths, and we are only at the very beginning of the maze into which they might lead the unwary, the rash or the enthusiastic. Our main concern is language; and the development of the language learner's abilities, capacities, competence and skills. Language starts with words. Words soon lead to phrases and sentences. Expression urgently needs to go beyond simple identification and reference—it becomes ideational and can move rapidly into abstract realms. Over a century ago, the French grammarian, Michel Breal, announced, 'A language does not consist exclusively of words: it consists of groups of words and of phrases.' And, he continued, 'It is not the word that forms a distinct unity for our mind: it is the idea.' (Quoted in Aarsleff, 1982:389.)

Ideas are vital to human expression: they are determiners of human liberty, of choice in response, and of individuality. Any text, of any kind, which encourages or invites interaction with the world of ideas—and consequently with the world of representational language—is a text that affirms, confirms and expands the indispensable human capacity to read the world.

SOURCES

The unidentified brief quotations used are, in order, from the following texts (Penguin editions unless otherwise indicated).

Preamble
"40 - Love" by Roger McGough, from GIG (1973) used by permission of the author; "The Fly,"by William Blake, from *Songs of Innocence and Experience* (1791).

Chapter 4
Noel Coward, *Blithe Spirit*, Act II (Eyre Methuen) in *Coward: Plays Four*, p.50; P.G. Wodehouse, *The Inimitable Jeeves*, p.130; Wodehouse, *ibid.*, p.218; C.H.B. Kitchin, *Death of My Aunt* (Hogarth Press) p.131; Elizabeth Bowen, 'The Visitor' in *Collected Stories*, p.127; James Joyce, *Ulysses*, p.57; Evelyn Waugh, *Vile Bodies*, p.63; R.S. Surtees, *Mr Sponge's Sporting Tour* (OUP World's Classics) p.117; Emma Tennant, *The Last of the Country House Murders* (Faber) p.66; Michael Innes, *The Ampersand Papers*, p.18.

Chapter 5, 1ˢᵗ quotations

Oscar Wilde, *Lady Windermere's Fan*, Act 3; William Shakespeare, *Titus Andronicus*, Act 1; a nursery rhyme; Rudyard Kipling, *The Ballad of East and West*; Kipling, from a speech; William Wordsworth, title of poem; William Shakespeare, *Much Ado About Nothing*, Act 3; Ogden Nash, *Reflection on Ice-Breaking*; George Mikes, *How to Be an Alien*; Robert Burton, *Anatomy of Melancholy*; William Blake, *The School-Boy*; Noel Coward, *Private Lives*, Act 1 (Eyre Methuen) in *Coward: Plays Two*, p.32.

Chapter 5, 2nd quotations
Oscar Wilde: *Lady Windermere's Fan*, Act 1; *The Picture of Dorian Gray*, p.90; quoted in Rutledge, L.W. (ed.) (1988) *Unnatural Quotations* (Boston: Alyson) p49; *The Decay of Lying*; *The Ballad of Reading Gaol*; *A Woman of No Importance*, Act 1; *The Importance of Being Earnest*, Act 3; *The Picture of Dorian Gray*, p.14; *ibid.*, p.29; *The Critic* as *Artist*. Remy de Gourmont, in Rutledge (ed.) *op. cit.*, p.71; Anita Loos, title of novel; Lord Byron, in Rutledge (ed.) *op. cit.*, p.148; Lord Acton, *Historical Essays and Studies*; Acton, *ibid.*; George Orwell, *Animal Farm*; George Orwell, *Nineteen Eighty-Four*; William Shakespeare, *King Henry IV, Part One*, Act 1; Robert Louis Stevenson, *Virginibus Puerisque*; William Makepeace Thackeray, *The Book of Snobs*.

Chapter 6, 1st quotations
Jonathan Keates (1983), 'Morn Advancing' in *Allegro Postillions* (Edinburgh: Salamander Press) (New York: George Braziller, 1985, p.26.)

Chapter 6, 2nd quotations
Ambrose Bierce, *The Disinterested Arbiter*.

Chapter 7, 1st quotations
Proverbial tongue-twister; song from the First World War; Alfred, Lord Tennyson, 'The Lotos-Eaters'; John Keats, 'Ode to a Nightingale'; Tennyson, 'Break, break, break'; Tennyson 'Rizpah';

John Dryden, 'Alexander's Feast'; Walt Whitman, 'When Lilacs Last in the Dooryard Bloom'd'.

Chapter 7, 2nd quotations

Overheard; Colin Dexter, *The Secret of Annexe Three* (Macmillan) p.41; Walt Whitman, 'The Wound-Dresser'; overheard; Joe Orton, *Loot* (Penguin New Dramatists no.3) p.82; Margaret Thatcher, from a speech quoted in *The Guardian*, 13th October 1984, and in Wales, 1989:23; overheard; P.G. Wodehouse, *Aunts Aren't Gentlemen*, p.103; Wodehouse, *ibid.*, p.86; Noel Coward, *Private Lives*, Act 1 (Eyre Methuen) in *Coward: Plays Two*, p.33.

Chapter 7, 3rd quotations

Invented, until 'Daphne. . .' which is from Ruth Rendell, *Vanity Dies Hard* (Arrow) p.41; then, Kate Chopin, *The Awakening* (The Women's Press) p.33; Margaret Yorke, *Devil's Work* (Arrow) p.120; Miles Franklin, My *Brilliant Career* (Virago) p.178; Forrest Reid, *Uncle Stephen* (GMP) p.80; George Orwell, *Nineteen Eighty-Four*, p.6; Iris Murdoch, *The Book and the Brotherhood* (Chatlo and Windus) p.307; Penelope Lively, *Moon Tiger*, p.111; Bruce Chatwin, *On the Black Hill* (Picador) p.42; Dirk Bogarde, *Voices in the Garden*, p.303.

Chapter 7, 4th quotations

John Buchan, *The Three Hostages*, p.97; Jeremy Beadle, *Death Scene* (GMP) p.124.

D.H. Lawrence, *Mother and Daughter*; Lawrence, *You Touched Me*; Lawrence, *The Man Who Loved Islands*.

BIBLIOGRAPHY

I feel that in the present context it is not the purpose of a bibliography either to give an exhaustive list of scientific writings which the reader will never wish to consult, or to demonstrate the range of the author's own reading. Rather, I hope, it will be more useful to the reader to provide sources for direct references made in the text, a few indications of helpful materials outside the normal range of language teaching methodology, and a select list of textbooks which offer well-presented representational materials suitable for L2 learners. (Where a book contains a full, useful bibliography, I have indicated this in parentheses.)

References

Aarsleff, H. (1982) *From Locke to Saussure: Essays on the Study of Language and Intellectual History* (London: Athlone).

Aston, G. (1991) 'Prabhu and after: communicative language teaching from angling to topiary', in M.T. Prat Zagrebelsky (ed.), *The Study of English Language in Italian Universities*, (Alessandria: Dell 'Orso).

Auden, W.H. (1968) *Secondary Worlds* (London: Faber).

Barthes, R. (1973; trans. R. Miller, 1975) *The Pleasure of the Text* (New York: Hill and Wang).

Barthes, R. (1977; trans. S. Heath, 1977) *Image-Music- Text* (London: Fontana).

Birch D. and M. O'Toole (eds.) (1988) *Functions of Style* (London: Pinter).

Brewer, D. (1984) *Childe Roland to the Dark Tower Came: An Approach to English Studies* (Cambridge: Cambridge University Press).

Brumfit, C.J. (1985) *Language and Literature Teaching: from Practice to Principle* (Oxford: Pergamon).

Carter, R. (1987) *Vocabulary: Applied Linguistic Perspectives* (London: Allen and Unwin). (Contains an excellent bibliography.)

Carter, R. and M.N. Long (1987) *The Web of Words: Exploring Literature through Language* (Cambridge: Cambridge University Press).

Carter, R. and M. McCarthy (eds.) (1988) *Vocabulary and Language Teaching* (London: Longman). (Contains an excellent bibliography.)

Connor, S. (1985) *Charles Dickens* (Oxford: Blackwell).

Culler, J. (1977) 'Structuralism and Literature' in H. Schiff (ed.) *Contemporary Approaches to English Studies* (London: Heinemann).

Eagleton, T. (1983) *Literary Theory: An Introduction* (Oxford: Blackwell).

Eco, U. (1979) *The Role of the Reader* (Bloomington: Indiana University Press).

Halliday, M.A.K. (1978) *Language as Social Semiotic: The Social Interpretation of Language and Meaning* (London: Edward Arnold).

Halliday, M.A.K. (1985: 2nd edn. 1989) *Spoken and Written Language* (Oxford: Oxford University Press).

Hawkes, T. (1986) *That Shakespeherian Rag: Essays on a Critical Process* (London: Methuen).

Hedge, T. (1985) *Using Readers in Language Teaching* (London: Macmillan).

Jakobson, R. (1960) 'Linguistics and Poetics', reprinted in D. Lodge (ed.) (1988) *Modern Criticism and Theory: A Reader* (London: Longman).

Kermode, F. (1957) *Romantic Image* (London: Routledge and Kegan Paul).

Krashen, S. (1981) *Second Language Acquisition and Second Language Learning* (Oxford: Pergamon).

Krashen S. (1982) *Principles and Practices of Second Language Acquisition* (Oxford: Pergamon).

Krashen, S. (1985) *The Input Hypothesis: Issues and Implications* (London: Longman).

Kress, G. (1988) 'Textual matters: The social effective of style' in D. Birch and M. O'Toole (eds.) *Functions of Style* (London: Pinter).

Lakoff, G. and M. Johnson (1980) *Metaphors We Live By* (Chicago: University of Chicago Press).

Leech, G. (1974) *Semantics* (Harmondsworth: Penguin).

Leech, G.N. and M.H. Short (1981) *Style in Fiction: A Linguistic Introduction to English Fictional Prose* (London: Longman).

Lodge, D. (1988) *Nice Work* (London: Sidgwick and Jackson).

Lodge, D. (ed.) (1988) *Modern Criticism and Theory: A Reader* (London: Longman).

Maley, A. and S. Moulding (1985) *Poem into Poem: Reading and Writing Poems with Students of English* (Cambridge: Cambridge UniversityPress).

Michaels, L. and C. Ricks (eds.) (1980) *The State of the Language* (Berkeley: University of California Press).

Nation, P. and J. Coady (1988) 'Vocabulary and Reading' in R. Carter and M. McCarthy (eds.) *Vocabulary and Language Teaching* (London: Longman).

Prabhu, N.S. (1987) *Second Language Pedagogy* (Oxford: Oxford University Press).

Quirk, R. (1980) 'Sound Barriers and Gangbangsprache' in L. Michaels and C. Ricks (eds.) *The State of the Language* (Berkeley: University of California Press).

Schiff, H. (ed.) (1977) *Contemporary Approaches to English Studies* (London: Heinemann).

Sperber, D. and D. Wilson (1986) *Relevance: Communication and Cognition* (Oxford: Blackwell).

Steiner, G. (1968) *Language and Silence* (London: Faber).

Underhill, A. (1989) 'Process in humanistic education' in *EL T journal* 43/4. Wales, K. (1989) *A Dictionary of Stylistics* (London: Longman). (Contains an excellent bibliography.)

Widdowson, H.G. (1975) *Stylistics and the Teaching of Literature* (London: Longman).

Widdowson, H.G. (1984) *Explorations in Applied Linguistics 2*, especially Section Four (pp.137 -173) (Oxford: Oxford University Press). (Contains an excellent bibliography.)

Williams, R. (1977) *Marxism and Literature* (Oxford: Oxford University Press).

Further reading

Aston, G. (1988) *Learning Comity* (Bologna: CLUEB).

Birch, D. (1989) *Language, Literature and Critical Practice* (London: Routledge and Kegan Paul).

Brinton, D.M., M.A. Snow and M.B. Wesche (1989) *Content-Based Second Language Instruction* (New York: Newbury House).

Brumfit, C.J. (ed.) (1983) *Teaching Literature Overseas: Language-Based Approaches* (ELT Documents 115) (Oxford: Pergamon/British Council).

Brumfit, C.J. (ed.) (1991) *Assessment in Literature Teaching* (Basingstoke: Macmillan). .

Brumfit, C.J. and R.A. Carter (eds.) (1986) *Literature and Language Teaching* (Oxford: Oxford University Press). (Contains an excellent bibliography.)

Carrell, P., J. Devine and D. Eskey (eds.) (1988) *Interactive Approaches to Second Language Reading* (Cambridge: Cambridge University Press).

Carter, R. (ed.) (1982) *Language and Literature: An Introductory Reader in Stylistics* (London: Allen and Unwin).

Carter, R. and D. Burton (eds.) (1982) *Literary Text and Language Study* (London: Edward Arnold).

Carter, R. and M. Long (1991) *Teaching Literature* (London: Longman). (Contains an excellent bibliography.)

Carter, R. and P. Simpson (eds.) (1988) *Language, Discourse and Literature: An Introductory Reader in Discourse Stylistics* (London: Unwin Hyman).

Carter, R.A., R. Walker and C.J. Brumfit (eds.) (1989) *Literature and the Learner: Methodological Approaches* (ELT Documents 130) (London: MEP Macmillan/British Council).

Chapman, R. (1973) *Linguistics and Literature: An Introduction to Literary Stylistics* (London: Edward Arnold).

Ching, M.K.L., M.C. Haley and R.F. Lunsford (eds.) (1980) *Linguistic Perspectives on Literature* (London: Routledge and Kegan Paul).

Cluysenaar, A. (1976) *Introduction to Literary Stylistics* (London: Batsford).

Collie, J. and S. Slater (1987) *Literature in the Language Classroom: A Resource Book of Ideas and Activities* (Cambridge: Cambridge University Press).

Cook, G. (1989) *Discourse* (Oxford: Oxford University Press).

Crystal, D. and D. Davy (1969) *Investigating English Style* (London: Longman).

Culler, J. (1975) *Structuralist Poetics: Structuralism, Linguistics, and the Study of Literature* (London: Routledge and Kegan Paul).

Culler, J. (1988) *On Puns* (Oxford: Blackwell).

D'haen, T. (ed.) (1986) *Linguistics and the Study of Literature* (Amsterdam: Rodopi).

Durant, A. and N. Fabb (1990), *Literary Studies in Action* (London: Routledge and Kegan Paul).

Eco, U. (1984) *Semiotics and the Philosophy of Language* (London: Macmillan).

Ellis, G. and J. McRae (eds.) (1991) *The Extensive Reading Handbook for Secondary Teachers* (Harmondsworth: Penguin).

Ellis, R. (1986) *Understanding Second Language Acquisition* (Oxford: Oxford University Press).

Fish, S. (1980) *Is There a Text in This Class? The Authority of Interpretive Communities* (Cambridge, Mass.: Harvard University Press).

Garvie, E. (1990) *Story as Vehicle: Teaching English to Young Children* (Garvie: Multilingual Matters).

Greenwood, J. (1988) *Class Readers* (Oxford: Oxford University Press).

Grellet, F. (1981) *Developing Reading Skills* (Cambridge: Cambridge University Press).

Halliday, MAK. (1973) *Explorations in the Functions of Language* (London: Edward Arnold).

Halliday, M.A.K. and R. Hasan (1976) *Cohesion in English* (London: Longman).

Hasan, R. (1985; 2nd edn. 1989) *Linguistics, Language, and Verbal Art* (Oxford: Oxford University Press).

Hawkes, T. (1977) *Structuralism and Semiotics* (London: Methuen).

Hawkes, T. (1972) *Metaphor* (London: Methuen).

Hawthorn, J. (1977) *Unlocking the Text* (London: Edward Arnold).

Hill, J. (1986) *Using Literature in Language Teaching* (London: Macmillan).

Holden, S. (ed.) (1988) *Literature and Language: The British Council 1987 Sorrento Conference* (Oxford: MEP/British Council).

Iser, W. (1974) *The Implied Reader* (Baltimore: johns Hopkins University Press).

Lodge, D. (1977) *The Modes of Modern Writing: Metaphor, Metonymy, and the Typology of Modern Literature* (London: Edward Arnold).

Lyons, J. (1981) *Language, Meaning and Context* (London: Fontam).

Malamah-Thomas, A. (1987) *Classroom Interaction* (Oxford: Oxford University Press).

Maley, A. and A. Duff (1990) *Literature* (Oxford: Oxford University Press).

Marckwardt, A.H (1978) *The Place of Literature in the Teaching of English* as a *Second or Foreign Language* (Honolulu: University Press of Hawaii).

Mclaughlin, B. (1987) *Theories of Second-Language Learning* (London: Edward Arnold).

Nuttall, C. (1982) *Reading Skills in a Foreign Language* (London: Heinemann).

Quirk, R. and H.G. Widdowson (eds.) (1985) *English in the World: Teaching and Learning the Language and Literatures* (Cambridge: Cambridge University Press/British Council).

Short, M. (ed.) (1989) *Reading, Analysing and Teaching Literature* (London: Longman).

Smith, F. (1978) *Reading* (Cambridge: Cambridge University Press).

Stern, H.H. (1983) *Fundamental Concepts of Language Teaching* (Oxford: Oxford University Press).

Stevick, E.W. (1990) *Humanism in Language Teaching* (Oxford: Oxford University Press).

Stubbs, M. (1980) *Language and Literacy* (London: Routledge and Kegan Paul).

Traugott, E.C. and M.L. Pratt (1980) *Linguistics for Students of Literature* (New York: Harcourt Brace Jovanovich).

Ur, P. (1981) *Discussions That Work* (Cambridge: Cambridge University Press).

Widdowson, H.G. (1972) 'On the deviance of literary discourse' in *Style* 6/3.

Widdowson, H.G. (1983) *Learning Purpose and Language Use* (Oxford: Oxford University Press).

Williams, E. (1984) *Reading in the Language Classroom* (London: Macmillan).

Wright, A, D. Betteridge and M. Buckby (1979) *Games for Language Learning* (Cambridge: Cambridge University Press).

Books containing representational materials

(Titles marked * also have a separate Teacher's Book; titles marked + are accompanied by cassettes.)

*+ Carter, R. and M.N. Long (1987) *The Web of Words: Exploring Literature through Language* (Cambridge: Cambridge University Press).

Clarke, D.F. (1989) *Talk About Literature* (London: Edward Arnold).

Cummings, M. and R. Simmons (1983) *The Language of Literature* (Oxford: Pergamon).

Gower, R. and M. Piercy (1987) *Reading Literature* (London: Longman).

Hart, C. (ed.) (1990) *Asterix and the English Language* (2 vols.) (London: Edward Arnold).

+ Hunter, J. and J. McRae (eds.) (1991) *Talking Texts: School and School days* (Harmondsworth: Penguin).

+ Hunter, J. and J. McRae (eds.) (1991) *Talking Texts: Oscar – The Importance of Being Wilde* (Harmondsworth: Penguin).

Knight, M. (ed.) (1981; 2nd edn. 1985) *Keep in Touch* (Oxford: Pergamon).

+ Mackay, R. (ed.) (1987) *Poems* (Oxford: MEP).

Maley, A. and A. Duff (1989) *The Inward Ear: Poetry in the Language* Classroom (Cambridge: Cambridge University Press).

+ Maley, A. and S. Moulding (1985) *Poem into Poem: Reading and Writing Poems with Students of English* (Cambridge: Cambridge University Press).

McRae, J. (1985) *Using Drama in the Classroom* (Oxford: Pergamon).

* + McRae, J. (1991) *Wordsplay* (Basingstoke: Macmillan).

* + McRae, J. and R. Boardman (1984) *Reading Between the Lines* (Cambridge: Cambridge University Press).

* + McRae, J. and L. Pantaleoni (1985; 2nd edn. 1986) *Words* on *the Page* (Firenze/Oxford: La Nuova Italia/Oxford University Press).

+ McRae, J. and L. Pantaleoni (1990) *Chapter and Verse* (Oxford: Oxford University Press).

Shackleton, M. (ed.) (1986) *Double Act: Ten One-act Plays* on *Five Themes* (London: Edward Arnold).

Tomlinson, B. (1986) *Openings* (London: Lingual House).

Wiley, G. and M. Dunk (1985) *Integrated English* (Cambridge: Cambridge University Press).

ABOUT THE AUTHOR

John McRae worked in over 70 countries in a wide-ranging career covering teaching, writing, and theatre. He is the author of many significant books including *The Language of Poetry*, *Wordsplay*, *Using Drama in the Classroom*, and with Ronald Carter, both *The Routledge History of Literature in English* and *The Penguin Guide to English Literature*.

He retired in 2017 after 20-plus years as Special Professor of Language in Literature Studies at the University of Nottingham, UK, and now lives in London and works in theatre as a director, actor, and writer.